100 SMART Board™ LESSONS

TERMS AND CONDITIONS

IMPORTANT - PERMITTED USE AND WARNINGS - READ CAREFULLY BEFORE USING

Minimum specification:
- PC/Mac with a CD-ROM drive and at least 128 MB RAM
- Microsoft Office 2000 or higher
- Adobe® Reader®
- Interactive whiteboard
- Notebook™ software
- Facilities for printing and sound (optional)

PC:
- Pentium II 450 MHz processor
- Microsoft Windows 2000 SP4 or higher

Mac:
- 700 MHz processor (1 GHz or faster recommended)
- Mac OS X.4 or higher

For all technical support queries, please phone Scholastic Customer Services on 0845 6039091.

YEAR 1

Scottish Primary 2

CREDITS

Authors
Karen Mawer (English); Ann Montague-Smith (mathematics);
Sarah Carpenter (science); Rhona Dick (history);
Alan Rodgers and Angella Streluck (geography);
Heather Cromie (English and other foundation subjects)

Development Editor
Niamh O'Carroll

Editor
Nicola Morgan

Assistant Editor
Margaret Eaton

Illustrators
Jim Peacock (Notebook file illustrations), Jenny Tulip (Notebook file and book illustrations), Theresa Tibbetts (additional Notebook file illustrations)

Series Designer
Joy Monkhouse

Designers
Rebecca Male, Allison Parry, Andrea Lewis, Shelley Best, Melissa Leeke and Anna Oliwa

CD-ROM developed in association with
Q & D Multimedia

ACKNOWLEDGEMENTS

SMART Board™ and Notebook™ are registered trademarks of SMART Technologies Inc.

Microsoft Office, Word, Excel and PowerPoint are either registered trademarks or trademarks of Microsoft Corporation in the United States and/or other countries.

With grateful thanks for advice, help and expertise to Angus McGarry (Trainer) and Fiona Ford (Education Development Consultant) at Steljes Ltd.

All Flash activities designed and developed by Q & D Multimedia.

Interactive Teaching Programs (developed by the Primary National Strategy) © Crown copyright.

Extracts from the Primary National Strategy's *Primary Framework for literacy and mathematics* (2006) www.standards.dfes.gov.uk/primaryframework © Crown copyright. Reproduced under the terms of the Click Use Licence.

Extracts from The National Literacy Strategy and The National Numeracy Strategy © Crown copyright. Material from the National Curriculum © The Queen's Printer and Controller of HMSO. Reproduced under the terms of HMSO Guidance Note 8.

Extracts from the QCA Scheme of Work © Qualifications and Curriculum Authority.

Every effort has been made to trace copyright holders for the works reproduced in this book, and the publishers apologise for any inadvertent omissions.

Designed using Adobe InDesign.

Published by Scholastic Ltd
Villiers House
Clarendon Avenue
Leamington Spa
Warwickshire CV32 5PR

www.scholastic.co.uk

Printed by Bell and Bain Ltd, Glasgow

1 2 3 4 5 6 7 8 9   7 8 9 0 1 2 3 4 5 6

Text © 2007 Karen Mawer (English);
Ann Montague-Smith (mathematics);
Sarah Carpenter (science); Rhona Dick (history);
Alan Rodgers and Angella Streluck (geography);
Heather Cromie (English and other foundation subjects)

© 2007 Scholastic Ltd

British Library Cataloguing-in-Publication Data
A catalogue record for this book is available from the British Library.

ISBN 978-0439-94537-0

The rights of the authors of this work have been asserted by them in accordance with the Copyright, Designs and Patents Act 1988.

CONTENTS

100 SMART BOARD™ LESSONS

Interactive whiteboards are fast becoming the must-have resource in today's classroom as they allow teachers to facilitate children's learning in ways that were inconceivable a few years ago. The appropriate use of interactive whiteboards, whether used daily in the classroom or once a week in the ICT suite, will encourage active participation in lessons and should increase learners' determination to succeed. Interactive whiteboards make it easier for teachers to bring subjects across the curriculum to life in new and exciting ways.

'There is a whiteboard revolution in UK schools.'
(Primary National Strategy)

What can an interactive whiteboard offer?

For the **teacher**, an interactive whiteboard offers the same facilities as an ordinary whiteboard, such as drawing, writing and erasing. However, the interactive whiteboard also offers many other possibilities to:
- save any work created during a lesson
- prepare as many pages as necessary
- display any page within the Notebook™ file to review teaching and learning
- add scanned examples of the children's work to a Notebook file
- change colours of shapes and backgrounds instantly
- use simple templates and grids
- link Notebook files to spreadsheets, websites and presentations.

Using an interactive whiteboard in the simple ways outlined above can enrich teaching and learning in a classroom, but that is only the beginning of the whiteboard's potential to educate and inspire.

For the **learner**, the interactive whiteboard provides the opportunity to share learning experiences, as lessons can be delivered with sound, still and moving images, and websites. Interactive whiteboards can be used to cater for the needs of all learning styles:
- kinaesthetic learners benefit from being able to physically manipulate images
- visual learners benefit from being able to watch videos, look at photographs and see images being manipulated
- auditory learners benefit from being able to access audio resources such as voice recordings and sound effects.

With a little preparation all of these resource types could be integrated in one lesson, a feat that would have been almost impossible before the advent of the interactive whiteboard!

Access to an interactive whiteboard

In schools where learners have limited access to an interactive whiteboard the teacher must carefully plan lessons in which the children will derive most benefit from using it. As teachers become familiar with the whiteboard they will learn when to use it and, importantly, when not to use it!

Where permanent access to an interactive whiteboard is available, it is important that the teacher plans the use of the board effectively. It should be used only in ways that will enhance or extend teaching and learning. Children still need to gain practical first-hand experience of many things. Some experiences cannot be recreated on an interactive whiteboard but others cannot be had without it. *100 SMART Board™ Lessons* offers both teachers and learners the most accessible and creative uses of this most valuable resource.

About the series

100 SMART Board™ Lessons is designed to reflect best practice in using interactive whiteboards. It is also designed to support all teachers in using this valuable tool by providing lessons and other resources that can be used on a whiteboard with little or no preparation. These inspirational lessons cover all National Curriculum subjects. They are perfect for all levels of experience and are an essential for any SMART Board users.

Safety note: Avoid looking directly at the projector beam as it is potentially damaging to eyes, and never leave the children unsupervised when using the interactive whiteboard.

Introduction

About the book

This book is divided into four chapters. Each chapter contains lessons and photocopiable activity sheets covering:

- English
- Mathematics
- Science
- Foundation subjects.

At the beginning of each chapter a **planning grid** identifies the title, the objectives covered and any relevant cross-curricular links in each lesson. Objectives are taken from the relevant Primary National Strategy, National Curriculum Programmes of Study (PoS), or the QCA Schemes of Work. All of the lessons should therefore fit into your existing medium-term plans. The planning grids have been provided in Microsoft Word format on the CD-ROM for this purpose.

Lesson plans

The lessons have a consistent structure with a starter activity, activities for shared and independent work, and a plenary to round up the teaching and learning and identify any assessment opportunities. Crucially, each lesson plan identifies resources required (including photocopiable activity sheets 🄿 and Notebook files that are provided on the CD-ROM 💿). Also highlighted are the whiteboard tools that could be used in the lesson.

Photocopiable activity sheets at the end of each chapter support the lessons. These sheets provide opportunities for group or individual work to be completed away from the board, but link to the context of the whiteboard lesson. They also provide opportunities for whole-class plenary sessions in which children discuss and present their work.

Two general record sheets are provided on pages 170 and 171. These are intended to support the teacher in recording ways in which the interactive whiteboard is used, and where and how interactive resources can be integrated into a lesson.

What's on the CD-ROM?

The accompanying CD-ROM provides an extensive bank of Notebook files. These support, and are supported by, the lessons in this book. As well as texts and images, a selection of Notebook files include the following types of files:

- Embedded Microsoft Office files: These include Microsoft Word and Excel documents. The embedded files are launched from the Notebook file and will open in their native Microsoft application.

- Embedded interactive files: These include specially commissioned interactive files as well as Interactive Teaching Programs (ITPs) from the Primary National Strategy.

- Printable PDF versions of the photocopiable activity and record sheets, as well as the answers to the mathematics activities, are also provided on the CD-ROM.

- 'Build your own' files: This contains a blank Notebook page with a bank of selected images and interactive tools from the Gallery, as well as specially commissioned images. It is supported by lesson plans in the book to help you to build your own Notebook files.

Introduction

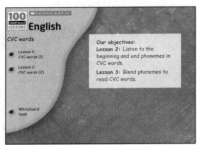

The Notebook files

All of the Notebook files have a consistent structure as follows:

Title and objectives page

Use this page to highlight the focus of the lesson. You might also wish to refer to this page at certain times throughout the lesson or at the end of the lesson to assess whether the learning objective was achieved.

Starter activity

This sets the context to the lesson and usually provides some key questions or learning points that will be addressed through the main activities.

Main activities

These activities offer independent, collaborative group, or whole-class work. The activities draw on the full scope of Notebook software and the associated tools, as well as the SMART Board tools.

What to do boxes are also included in many of the prepared Notebook files. These appear as tabs in the top right-hand corner of the screen. To access these notes, simply pull out the tabs to reveal planning information, additional support and key learning points.

Plenary

A whole-class activity or summary page is designed to review work done both at the board and away from the board. In many lessons, children are encouraged to present their work.

Whiteboard tools page

The whiteboard tools page gives a reminder of the tools used in the lesson and provides instructions on how they are used.

HOW TO USE THE CD-ROM

Setting up your screen for optimal use

It is best to view the Notebook pages at a screen display setting of 1280 × 1024 pixels. To alter the screen display, select Settings, then Control Panel from the Start menu. Next, double-click on the Display icon and then click on the Settings tab. Finally, adjust the Screen area scroll bar to 1280 × 1024 pixels. Click on OK.

If you prefer to use a screen display setting of 800 × 600 pixels, ensure that your Notebook view is set to 'Page Width'. To alter the view, launch Notebook and click on View. Go to Zoom and select the 'Page Width' setting. If you use a screen display setting of 800 × 600 pixels, text in the prepared Notebook files may appear larger when you edit it on screen.

Viewing the printable resources

Adobe® Reader® is required to view the printable resources. All the printable resources are PDF files.

Visit the Adobe® website at **www.adobe.com** to download the latest version of Adobe® Reader®.

Introduction

Getting started

The program should run automatically when you insert the CD-ROM into your CD drive. If it does not, use My Computer to browse to the contents of the CD-ROM and click on the *100 SMART Board™ Lessons* icon.

When the program starts, you are invited to register the product either online or using a PDF registration form. You also have the option to register later. If you select this option, you will be taken, via the Credits screen, to the Main menu.

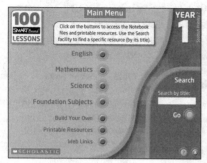

Main menu

The Main menu divides the Notebook files by subject: English, mathematics, science and foundation subjects. Clicking on the appropriate blue button for any of these options will take you to a separate Subject menu (see below for further information). The 'Build your own' file is also accessed through the Main menu (see below). The activity sheets are provided in separate menus. To access these resources, click on Printable resources.

Individual Notebook files or pages can be located using the search facility by keying in words (or part words) from the resource titles in the Search box. Press Go to begin the search. This will bring up a list of the titles that match your search.

The Web Links button takes you to a list of useful web addresses. A help button 📍 is included on all menu screens. The Help notes on the CD-ROM provide a range of general background information and technical support for all users.

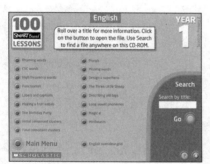

Subject menu

Each Subject menu provides all of the prepared Notebook files for each chapter of the book. Roll over each Notebook file title to reveal a brief description of the contents in a text box at the top of the menu screen; clicking on the blue button will open the Notebook file. Click on Main menu to return to the Main menu screen.

'Build your own' file

Click on this button to open a blank Notebook page and a collection of Gallery objects, which will be saved automatically into the My Content folder in the Gallery. You only need to click on this button the first time you wish to access the 'Build your own' file, as the Gallery objects will remain in the My Content folder on the computer on which the file was opened. To use the facility again, simply open a blank Notebook page and access the images and interactive resources from the same folder under My Content. If you are using the CD-ROM on a different computer you will need to click on the 'Build your own' button again.

Printable resources

The printable PDF activity sheets are also divided by chapter. Click on the subject to find all the activity sheets related to that subject/chapter. The answers to Chapter 2, mathematics, are also provided.

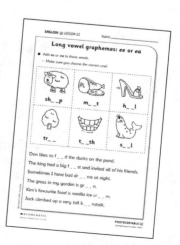

To alternate between the menus on the CD-ROM and other open applications, hold down the Alt key and press the Tab key to switch to the desired application.

English

The lessons in the English chapter match the objectives in the Primary National Strategy's *Primary Framework for literacy*. These objectives are listed in the curriculum grid below, along with the corresponding objectives from the medium-term planning in the National Literacy Strategy. The curriculum grids in this book are also provided on the accompanying CD-ROM, in editable format, to enable you to integrate the lessons into your planning. The lessons show how the interactive whiteboard can be used to share and introduce new ideas, and actively involve the children in their learning.

Lesson title	PNS objectives	NLS objectives	Expected prior knowledge	Cross-curricular links
Lesson 1: Rhyming words 💿 🄿	Word recognition	W1: To practise and secure the ability to rhyme.	• Be able to hear when words rhyme.	Art and design QCA Unit 1B 'Investigating materials' Citizenship QCA Unit 3 'Animals and us'
Lesson 2: CVC words (1) 💿 🄿	Word structure and spelling • Segment sounds into their constituent phonemes in order to spell them correctly.	W3: To practise and secure the ability to hear phonemes in CVC words. W4: To discriminate and segment all three phonemes in CVC words.	• Recognise all letters of the alphabet. • The sound for each letter of the alphabet.	There are no specific links for this lesson.
Lesson 3: CVC words (2) 💿	Word recognition • Apply phonic knowledge as the prime approach to reading and spelling unfamiliar words that are not completely decodable.	W5: To blend phonemes to read CVC words. W6: To represent in writing the three phonemes in CVC words.	• The sound for each letter of the alphabet. • How to write all letters of the alphabet.	There are no specific links for this lesson.
Lesson 4: Colour words 💿 🄿	Word recognition • Recognise automatically an increasing number of high frequency words.	W8: To read on sight other familiar words (colour words).	• How to read simple CVC words. • Colour names.	Art and design PoS (4a) Pupils should be taught about visual elements, including colour.
Lesson 5: Reading high frequency words 💿	Word recognition • Recognise automatically an increasing number of high frequency words.	W9: To read on sight approximately 30 high frequency words identified for Y1 and Y2.	• How to read simple CVC words and the first 45 words from the YR list.	Mathematics PNS: Understanding shape
Lesson 6: Jumbled sentences	Sentence structure and punctuation • Compose and write simple sentences independently to communicate meaning.	S4: To write captions and simple sentences and to re-read, recognising whether or not they make sense.	• How to write simple words. • How to read own writing.	Mathematics PNS: Counting and understanding number
Lesson 7: Capital letters 💿	Sentence structure and punctuation • Use capital letters and full stops when punctuating simple sentences.	S9: To use a capital letter for the personal pronoun 'I' and for the start of a sentence.	• How to form capital letters for all letters in the alphabet. • What a sentence is.	Geography QCA Unit 5 'Where in the world is Barnaby Bear?'
Lesson 8: Captions 💿	Sentence structure and punctuation • Compose and write simple sentences independently to communicate meaning.	T12: To read and use captions. T14: To write captions for their own work.	• How to read age-appropriate text. • How to write simple words. • Local area vocabulary.	Geography QCA Unit 1 'Around our school – the local area' ICT QCA Unit 1B 'Using a word bank'
Lesson 9: Making a list 💿 🄿	Creating and shaping texts • Convey information and ideas in simple non-narrative forms.	T13: To read and follow simple instructions. T15: To make simple lists for planning. T16: To write and draw simple instructions and labels.	• How to write simple words. • Fruit names.	Design and technology QCA Unit 1C 'Eat more fruit and vegetables' Art and design QCA Unit 2B 'Mother Nature, designer'
Lesson 10: Making a picture book 💿 🄿	Creating and shaping texts • Create short simple texts on paper and on screen that combine words with images.	T7: To re-enact stories in a variety of ways. T11: To make simple picture storybooks with sentences, modelling them on basic conventions.	• Be able to retell a story orally. • Parts of a book, for example the front cover, title and so on.	Art and design QCA Unit 2A 'Picture this!' Speaking and listening Objective 4: To explore familiar themes and characters through improvisation and role play.

Lesson title	PNS objectives	NLS objectives	Expected prior knowledge	Cross-curricular links
Lesson 11: Initial consonant clusters (1)	Word recognition Word structure and spelling	**W3:** To discriminate, read and spell words with initial consonant clusters (br, cr, dr, fr, gr, pr, tr).	• Recognise all letters of the alphabet. • The sound for each letter of the alphabet. • How to read and spell CVC words.	**Science** QCA Unit 1C 'Sorting and using materials' **ICT** QCA Unit 1D 'Labelling and classifying'
Lesson 12: Initial consonant clusters (2)	Word recognition Word structure and spelling	**W3:** To discriminate, read and spell words with initial consonant clusters (bl, cl, fl, gl, pl, sl).	• Recognise all letters of the alphabet. • The sound for each letter of the alphabet. • How to read and spell CVC words.	**Mathematics** PNS: Counting and understanding number
Lesson 13: Final consonant clusters	Word recognition Word structure and spelling	**W3:** To discriminate, read and spell words with final consonant clusters (st, sp, sk, nd, nt, nk).	• Recognise all letters of the alphabet • The sound for each letter of the alphabet • How to read and spell CVC words.	**Speaking and listening** Objective 2: To listen with sustained concentration. **Science** QCA Unit 1C 'Sorting and using materials'
Lesson 14: Spelling high frequency words	Word structure and spelling	**W9:** To spell common irregular words.	• How to spell simple CVC words and the first 45 words from the YR list.	General link to history, geography, science and mathematics.
Lesson 15: Plurals	Word structure and spelling	**W8:** To investigate and learn spellings of words with 's' for plurals.	• How to spell CVC, CCVC and CVCC words. • How to spell the first 45 words from the YR list.	**Mathematics** PNS: Counting and understanding number
Lesson 16: Missing words	Understanding and interpreting texts • Use syntax and context when reading for meaning.	**S3:** To predict words from preceding words in sentences and investigate the sorts of words that 'fit'.	• How to use picture clues and phonic strategies to decode unfamiliar words when reading.	**Citizenship** QCA Unit 2 'Choices'
Lesson 17: Full stops	Sentence structure and punctuation • Use capital letters and full stops when punctuating simple sentences.	**S5:** To continue demarcating sentences in writing, ending a sentence with a full stop.	• What a sentence is.	General link to history, geography and science.
Lesson 18: Design a superhero	Understanding and interpreting texts • Identify characters in stories, and find specific information in simple texts. Creating and shaping texts • Create short simple texts on paper that combine words with images. Text structure and organisation • Group written sentences together in chunks of meaning or subject.	**T8:** To identify and discuss characters. **T15:** To build simple profiles of characters from stories.	• What a character is. • Some superheroes and their characteristics.	**Citizenship** QCA Unit 4 'People who help us' **Design and technology** QCA Unit 1A 'Moving pictures'
Lesson 19: Retelling a story	Speaking • Retell stories, ordering events using story language. Text structure and organisation • Write chronological texts using simple structures.	**T4:** To retell stories, giving the main points in sequence. **T14:** To represent outlines of story plots using, for example, captions, pictures, arrows to record main incidents in order.	• How to retell a story orally.	**Design and technology** QCA Unit 1D 'Homes' **Art and design** QCA Unit 2C 'Can buildings speak?' **Speaking and listening** Objective 8: To act out well-known stories.
Lesson 20: Labelling body parts	Creating and shaping texts • Convey information and ideas in simple non-narrative forms. • Find and use new and interesting words.	**T22:** To write labels for drawings and diagrams.	• How to write simple words. • Names of body parts.	**Science** QCA Unit 1A 'Ourselves' **Art and design** QCA Unit 1A 'Self-portrait'

Lesson title	PNS objectives	NLS objectives	Expected prior knowledge	Cross-curricular links
Lesson 21: Describing old toys ⬤ 🅿	**Creating and shaping texts** • Convey information and ideas in simple non-narrative forms. • Find and use new and interesting words and phrases, including story language. • Create short simple texts on paper that combine words with images. **Sentence structure and punctuation** • Compose and write simple sentences independently to communicate meaning.	**T25:** To assemble information from own experience; to use simple sentences to describe, based on examples from reading; to organise information in lists.	• How to write simple sentences. • Technical vocabulary to describe toys.	**History** QCA Unit 1 'How are our toys different from those in the past?' **Science** QCA Unit 1C 'Sorting and using materials' **ICT** QCA Unit 1D 'Labelling and classifying'
Lesson 22: Long vowel phoneme *ee* ⬤ 🅿	**Word recognition** • Recognise/use alternative ways of spelling the phonemes already taught.	**W1:** To identify, blend and segment words containing the common spelling patterns for the long vowel phoneme *ee*.	• How to read and spell all single letter phonemes and consonant blends.	**ICT** QCA Unit 1C 'The information around us'
Lesson 23: Long vowel phoneme *oa* ⬤ 🅿	**Word recognition** • Recognise/use alternative ways of spelling the phonemes already taught.	**W1:** To identify, blend and segment words containing the common spelling patterns for the long vowel phoneme *oa*.	• How to read and spell all single letter phonemes and consonant blends.	**ICT** QCA Unit 1C 'The information around us'
Lesson 24: Long vowel phoneme *oo* ⬤ 🅿	**Word recognition** • Recognise/use alternative ways of spelling the phonemes already taught.	**W1:** To identify, blend and segment words containing the common spelling patterns for the long vowel phoneme *oo*.	• How to read and spell all single letter phonemes and consonant blends.	**ICT** QCA Unit 1C 'The information around us'
Lesson 25: Magic *e* ⬤ 🅿	**Word recognition** • Recognise/use alternative ways of spelling the phonemes already taught.	**W1:** To identify, blend and segment words containing the split digraph long vowel phonemes.	• How to read and spell all single letter phonemes and consonant blends. • The vowel letter names.	**ICT** QCA Unit 1C 'The information around us'
Lesson 26: Vowels and consonants	**Word recognition** • Recognise automatically an increasing number of high frequency words.	**W9:** To understand and use the terms *vowel* and *consonant*. **W2:** To read on sight high frequency words.	• The letters of the alphabet.	**Mathematics** PNS: Handling data **ICT** QCA Unit 1E 'Representing information graphically'
Lesson 27: Question marks ⬤	**Sentence structure and punctuation** • Use capital letters and full stops when punctuating simple sentences.	**S7:** To add question marks to questions. **T22:** To write simple questions.	• How to ask a question. • How to distinguish between a question and a statement.	**Science** PoS Sc1 (2a) Pupils should be taught to ask questions. **Speaking and listening** Objective 4: To explore characters through role play.
Lesson 28: Counting rhyme ⬤	**Creating and shaping texts** • Create short simple texts on paper that combine words with images.	**T15:** To use poems or parts of poems as a model for own writing.	• Number words. • How to rhyme.	**Mathematics** PNS: Counting and understanding number
Lesson 29: Finding answers ⬤ 🅿	**Understanding and interpreting texts** • Recognise the main elements that shape different texts. **Creating and shaping texts** • Convey information in simple non-narrative forms. **Sentence structure and punctuation** • Compose and write simple sentences independently to communicate meaning.	**T19:** To identify simple questions and use text to find answers; to locate parts of a text that give particular information.	• How to use range of strategies to read simple texts.	**Science** PoS Sc2: Life processes and living things
Lesson 30: Recount of planting a seed	**Understanding and interpreting texts** • Recognise the main elements that shape different texts. **Creating and shaping texts** • Convey information in simple non-narrative forms. **Sentence structure and punctuation** • Compose and write simple sentences independently to communicate meaning.	**T20:** To write simple recounts linked to topics of interest/study or to personal experience.	• How to write simple sentences. • How to use simple punctuation.	**Science** QCA Unit 1B 'Growing plants'

Rhyming words

Learning objective
PNS: Word recognition

Resources
'Rhymes' Notebook file;
photocopiable page 41
'Rhyming words', one copy for
each child, cut up and
mounted onto card and
laminated with punched-out
holes next to each word;
shoelaces (or similar) to thread
through the cards; writing
books and pencils.

Links to other subjects
Art and design
QCA Unit 1B 'Investigating
materials'
● Make a collage with
different materials to illustrate
one of the rhyming sentences
(such as *The cat sat in a hat*).
Citizenship
QCA Unit 3 'Animals and us'
● Link the work with
discussion about real animals,
in the wild and at home. Ask:
*Why are animals important?
How can we look after them?*

Starter
Open page 2 of the Notebook file. Explain that you are going to say two words, and ask the children to identify whether the words rhyme or not (for example *cat* and *mat*, or *cat* and *can*). Encourage a 'thumbs up' sign if they do rhyme and a 'thumbs down' sign if they don't. Ask the children for other examples of words that rhyme and assess their responses. Give the opportunity for a more confident learner to explain what *rhyme* means.

Whole-class shared work
● Go to page 3 and ask a more confident reader to read the first sentence clearly to the class.
● Encourage the children to find the rhyming words within the sentence and share them with a talking partner.
● Select one pair of children to use a Highlighter pen 🖊 to highlight the rhyming words. Ask the rest of the class: *Have they highlighted the correct words?*
● Point out that words that rhyme sound the same at the end and often have the same spelling of the word ending.
● Repeat this process for the other two sentences.
● Go to page 4 and ask what word goes with the picture. Move the spyglass beneath the picture to check.
● Read the words on the right-hand side with the children. Explain that one of the words on the right-hand side rhymes with *cat*. Ask the children to discuss with their talking partners which word they think it is. When pressed, the correct word will 'cheer'.
● Repeat this for pages 5 to 12.

Independent work
● Give out the rhyming word cards you have prepared (see Resources) and ask the children to read all of the words carefully.
● Demonstrate how to thread a shoelace through the holes to join rhyming words.
● When the children have completed the threading, encourage them to compare their answers with a talking partner and discuss any differences.
● Ask the children to write the pairs of rhyming words in their books, looking carefully at the spelling of them.
● Limit the number of words for less confident learners.
● As an extension challenge, ask children to think of another word that rhymes with the two they have already found.

Plenary
● Go to page 13. Make the word *cat* on the first line by dragging the *c* next to the *-at* rime and ask a child to read the word.
● Challenge the children to think of words that rhyme with *cat*. When a child thinks of a real word, allow them to drag the correct letter from the box and add it to one of the *-at* rimes to make the word.
● Read all of the words together and establish that they do rhyme.

Whiteboard tools
Use a Pen from the Pen tray
to make annotations and a
Highlighter pen to highlight
rhyming words.

 Pen tray

 Highlighter pen

 Select tool

Learning objective
PNS: Word structure and spelling
● Segment words into their constituent phonemes in order to spell them correctly.

Resources ⊙ ▣
'CVC words' Notebook file; photocopiable page 42 'CVC words', one for each child; a letter fan for each child containing every letter of the alphabet.

Links to other subjects
There are no specific links for this lesson.

CVC words (1)

Starter
Open page 2 of the Notebook file. Give each child a letter fan and explain how to use it. Say a letter sound and give the children time to locate and show it. Assess their level of understanding of sound-letter correspondence. Move on to ask them to show initial, final and medial sounds in CVC words as appropriate.

Whole-class shared work
● Go to page 3 and introduce the two characters, Billy and Kelly the Kind Fairy.
● Using pages 4 to 10, help the fairy to change 'man' into 'pet' by changing one phoneme in the word at a time.
● When the word is first displayed, say each phoneme separately then blend it together and say the whole word. Ask a child to identify the new word to be made from the picture clue on the right-hand side of the page.
● Encourage the children to choose which letter they need to change and what it should be changed to.
● Invite a volunteer to come to the whiteboard, select the correct letter and drag and drop it into the appropriate position in the word.
● Once the new word is made, say each phoneme separately, then blend it together and say the whole word. Ask: *Have we made the correct word?*
● Next, show the CVC words on pages 11 to 18 one at a time. Ask the children to work out what phoneme is missing from each of the words and show the answer using their letter fans.
● Invite a child to drag the correct letter into place on the whiteboard.

Independent work
● Give out copies of photocopiable page 42. Ensure that everyone knows what each picture shows.
● Tell the children that they must fill in the missing letter for each CVC word. Encourage them to say the word slowly and then segment it into the three phonemes.
● Display an alphabet to support forming letters correctly.
● To secure the ability to hear initial and final phonemes for less confident learners, give them a set of pictures or objects to sort by initial or final sounds.
● Extend more confident learners by asking them to put the words into simple sentences.

Plenary
● Go to page 19. Ask a child to segment the word into three phonemes by dragging them apart.
● Ask another child to say the three phonemes separately.
● Drag the three phonemes back together again to recreate the whole word and demonstrate how to blend the phonemes by saying them more quickly in order to read the word.
● Repeat this with pages 20 to 22, but ask the children to blend the phonemes and tell a partner what the word is before sharing the answer with the class.

Whiteboard tools
Use a Pen from the Pen tray to annotate the children's ideas.

 Pen tray

 Select tool

CVC words (2)

 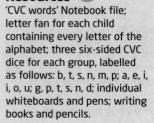
Starter
Display page 23 of the Notebook file. Discuss the different strategies that can be used for decoding an unfamiliar word. Focus on the suggestion that a word can be sounded out. Ask the children to explain what this means and how they would do it.

Go to page 24 and ask the children to read the sentences aloud. Discuss how they tackled any unfamiliar words.

Whole-class shared work
● Go to page 25 and explain that the children are going to find out how many real words they can make using the phoneme cards.
● Demonstrate how to say the separate phonemes in the word *tug* and then blend them together to read the whole word. Ask: *Is it a real word?* Clarify any misconceptions.
● Drag the *t* card into the bin and then ask the children to blend the next three phonemes displayed (f-u-g). Again, ask the children to decide whether the word is a real word or not.
● Next drag the *u* card into the bin and repeat the blending. Then drag the *g* card into the bin. Continue to remove cards in order (left to right) until you get to *pat*.
● Encourage the children to list real words on the page at the side of the bin.
● Provide the children with individual whiteboards and pens. Ask them to read the CVC words on page 26 and then choose three words that they think are real and write them on their boards.
● Discuss as a class and ask a volunteer to sort the words by dragging them into the correct columns on the Notebook page.

Independent work
● Give each similar ability group a set of three CVC dice (see Resources) and tell them to roll each one.
● They then put the dice into CVC order (dice may need to be colour-coded to support this).
● As a group, the children blend the phonemes and decide if they make a real word. They should list the real words in their writing books.
● Blend the VC rime for less confident learners, asking them only to add the initial consonant.
● Extend more confident learners by altering one of the consonant dice to show initial consonant blends, so they can blend CCVC words.

Plenary
● Go to page 27. Press on 'Word 1' to hear the word spoken aloud *(box)*. Ask the children to spell the word by dragging the correct letters up to the line.
● Check that the spelling is correct using the spyglass. Repeat with the second word.
● Give each child a letter fan. Say a CVC word to the children and ask them to make it with their letter fan. Ask one child with the correct answer on their fan to write the CVC word on the board. Assess which children need more support with spelling CVC words.
● Use page 28 to assess the children's understanding of CVC words.

Colour words

Learning objective
PNS: Word recognition
● Recognise automatically an increasing number of familiar high frequency words.

Resources
'High frequency words' Notebook file; photocopiable page 43 'Colour mixing', one for each child; coloured pens or pencils. Make sets of six cards for each child, each card showing two colours that can be mixed into a third colour (for example, red and yellow).

Links to other subjects
Art and design
PoS (4a) Pupils should be taught about visual elements, including colour.
● Extend the children's knowledge of colour mixing.

Starter
Ask the children to think of as many different colours as they can. Go to page 2 of the Notebook file. Get the children to point out any colour words that they recognise. Read the chant to them. Invite them to join in with the colour words. Explain that the colour of the words gives a clue to what the colour word says. Identify and highlight the rhymes in the chant.

Whole-class shared work
● Go to page 3 and ask the children to name the colours in turn. Allow a child to wipe off the paint with the Eraser from the Pen tray as the colour is named, to reveal the colour word underneath.
● Examine the colour words. Look at initial sounds and the shapes and spelling patterns within the words.
● Go to page 4 and ask the class to read the colour words and match them to the blobs of colour.
● Pages 5 to 8 extend the children's understanding of colour mixing as well as their colour word knowledge.
● Show page 5, read the colour sum and ask the children what the answer is. Demonstrate with ready-mix paint if the children are unsure.
● Drag the correct colour into place and read the whole sum. Then ask the children to drag the correct labels onto each colour.
● Repeat for pages 6 to 8.

Independent work
● Give out copies of photocopiable page 43 and the sets of prepared cards (see Resources).
● The children should pick a card and name the colours. Demonstrate how to colour the first two blobs in the colour sentence on their sheet to match the card.
● Ask the children to decide which new colour the two colours will make when they are mixed together and colour the third blob that colour.
● Encourage them to use the word bank at the top of the sheet to label the colours.
● Work with the less confident learners on pages 9 and 10 of the Notebook file to sort pictures of objects by their colour. Extend this by sorting real objects, adding the correct colour label to each group from a choice of three.
● Extend more confident learners by asking them to write colour sentences to make pink and grey (you will need to introduce the word 'white').

Plenary
● Take the children into the hall and stick different colour words on the walls with suitable gaps between.
● Ask the children to move around the hall in a variety of ways. When you say a colour word they must find it on the wall and sit down in front of it.
● Assess which children need more support in reading colour words.

Whiteboard tools
Use the Eraser from the Pen tray to wipe off the paint to reveal the colour words on page 3.

 Pen tray

 Highlighter pen

 Select tool

Reading high frequency words

Learning objective
PNS: Word recognition
● Recognise automatically an increasing number of familiar high frequency words.

Resources
'High frequency words' Notebook file; counters (20 per pair). Prepare a bingo board for each pair of children: a 5×4 grid with 20 high frequency words in different places. Prepare individual bingo cards of the same words.

Links to other subjects
Mathematics
PNS: Understanding shape
● Link the themes of shape and pattern (the shapes of words, and the pattern made in the 'word brick wall' activity in the whole-class shared work) to work in mathematics. Describe the word and letter shapes in terms of rectangles and squares, and make different tessellating patterns with rectangles and squares.

Starter

Display page 11 of the Notebook file and read the words with the children. Focus on the shape of the word and point out any tall letters. Explain that looking at the shape of a word can help you to recognise it. Challenge the children to match the word shapes to the words. Drag the shapes over the words to check their ideas. Enable the Screen Shade to show only the shapes and not the words. Challenge the children to recall which words belonged in each shape.

Whole-class shared work

● Read the sentences on page 12 together and discuss the strategies used to work out any unfamiliar words.
● Explain that the same sentences are written on the next pages but with a word missing. The correct spelling of the missing word must be chosen from a choice of four.
● Work through pages 13 to 16 and discuss which of the words are spelled correctly. Use the Eraser from the Pen tray to rub over the blank space in the sentence to reveal the correct spelling of the word.
● Use page 17 to assess children who have not yet contributed to the lesson. Ask a child to drag the first brick from the bottom right corner of the page and place it next to the word *here* to start building a wall.
● Ask the same child to read the word. They can 'ask the audience' if they are unsure.
● Continue this with different children until all the bricks have been used.

Independent work

● Give each pair of children a bingo board and 20 counters (see Resources).
● Read a word card to the class. Tell pairs to cover the word with a counter if it is on their board.
● Explain that they need to get a line of counters across the board to win the game, and that when they have done this they should call 'bingo'.
● Keep the called cards to one side so you can check the words that have been covered up on the winning team's card.
● Less confident learners will need to play this game in a small group with an adult supporting them.
● Encourage more confident learners to work in their own groups, with one child designated as the caller.

Plenary

● Enable the Spotlight tool. Go to page 18, and ask the children to use the spotlight to find the words hidden in the ocean (change the words if necessary to match the needs of the children).
● When they find a word, ask them to read it aloud. When they have found all of the words, ask a child to use the spotlight again to find a specific word.

Whiteboard tools
Use a Pen from the Pen tray or a Highlighter pen to make annotations, and the Spotlight tool and Screen Shade to focus on parts of the page.

 Pen tray

 Screen Shade

 Spotlight tool

 Select tool

Jumbled sentences

Starter
Tell the children that you are feeling very sleepy today and you need some help with your writing. Type a simple sentence on a blank Notebook page, missing out an obvious word (For example, *The dog is black white.*) Ask the children to read the sentence to check that you haven't made a mistake. Talk about whether the sentence makes sense, and ask them what you need to do to correct it.

Whole-class shared work
● Explain how important it is to check your own writing because it's easy to make mistakes.
● Show the children the first page of the prepared Notebook file (see Resources). Read the jumbled sentence and feign confusion.
● Say that you think the computer must have jumbled up the words in the sentence. Invite the children to help re-order the words in the sentence so that it makes sense.
● Ask: *Which word do you think will go first?* Give the children a clue by reminding them that sentences begin with a capital letter.
● Experiment with the order of the words. The children should soon realise that some word combinations don't work.
● Keep re-reading the sentence to ensure that it makes sense.
● Repeat this with the jumbled sentences on the other prepared pages.

Independent work
● Give a set of prepared cards to each group (see Resources). Explain that these jumbled sentences need to be re-ordered.
● Invite the children to choose a card and re-order the words to create a sentence that makes sense.
● Encourage them to keep re-reading the sentence to check it.
● Give less confident learners each word on a separate card so they can physically re-order the cards.
● Extend more confident learners by asking them to add a new word to the sentence to make it more interesting, while still making sense.

Plenary
● Give out large cards with a word from a simple sentence written on each one. Ask the children holding the cards to order themselves to create a sentence that makes sense.
● Ask: *Could any extra words be added to the sentence, or any of the words be replaced to make the sentence more interesting?*
● Discuss as a class why it is so important to re-read writing to check for errors.

Capital letters

Learning objective
PNS: Sentence structure and punctuation
● Use capital letters and full stops when punctuating simple sentences.

Resources
'Punctuation' Notebook file; Big Book; prepared cards showing simple sentences without capital letters; writing books and pencils.

Links to other subjects
Geography
QCA Unit 5 'Where in the world is Barnaby Bear?'
● As you look at different places and countries with the children, point out to them that these names also start with a capital letter. Encourage them to use capital letters for place and country names in their written work.

Starter
Open page 2 of the Notebook file. Look carefully at the letters and ask the children what they notice about them. Focus on the fact that some of the letters are lower case and some are upper case (or capital). Invite the children to sort the letters into either lower case or upper case by selecting them and dragging them to the correct set.

Whole-class shared work
● Ask the children where a capital letter can normally be found.
● Display page 3 and explain that a sentence always begins with a capital letter.
● Comment that the pronoun 'I' and the initial letters of people's names are also always capital.
● Read the sentences on page 4 with the children. Explain that they are sentences because they start with a capital letter, end with a full stop and make sense on their own.
● Encourage the children to look closely at the sentences to find the capital letters. Invite different volunteers to highlight them.
● Discuss why the capital letters have been used – for example, the beginning of a sentence, the initial letter of someone's name, the personal pronoun 'I'.
● Show the sentences on page 5 and comment that they are not correct because a robber has stolen all of the capital letters.
● Invite the children to replace the capital letters, explaining why they are needed in each case. Check the answers by pulling the screen across the sentences.

Independent work
● Give each group a set of prepared cards (see Resources).
● Tell the children to choose a card and re-write the sentence in their books with the capital letters in the correct place.
● Stop the children at various points and ask them to check what they have done so far, making sure that each sentence begins with a capital letter.
● Work with less confident learners to find and highlight capital letters in simple sentences. Help them to identify that capital letters are always at the beginning of a sentence.
● Extend more confident learners by asking them to write their own sentences about a given topic, using capital letters where appropriate.

Plenary
● Introduce the punctuation game to the children. Tell them they are going to read from a Big Book, and when they see a capital letter they must put both hands straight up in the air to make themselves tall like a capital letter.
● Extend the game further by telling them to stab the air with their index finger, as though they are making a full stop, when they see a full stop. Read the Big Book together at a steady pace, and add the actions.

Whiteboard tools
Use a Highlighter pen to highlight capital letters. Use the On-screen Keyboard, accessed through the Pen tray or the SMART Board tools menu, to type in missing capital letters.

 Pen tray

 Select tool

 Highlighter pen

 On-screen Keyboard

Captions

Learning objective
PNS: Sentence structure and punctuation
● Compose and write simple sentences independently to communicate meaning.

Resources
'Labels and captions' Notebook file; individual whiteboards and pens (one for each pair); display board showing photographs, maps and drawings of the local area collected while carrying out topic work.

Links to other subjects
Geography
QCA Unit 1 'Around our school – the local area'
ICT
QCA Unit 1B 'Using a word bank'
● Both the above objectives link to the work in this lesson.

Starter
Talk with the children about the ways that they travelled to school this morning, and what they saw on the way. Open page 2 of the Notebook file, read the captions together and talk about the pictures on the page. Ask: *Did anyone see any of these things on their way to school? Where did you see them? What were they there for?*

Whole-class shared work
● Display the pictures and captions on page 3. Explain that each picture has two captions, but that the captions are not in order.
● Read each of the captions carefully with the children. Ask them to discuss with a friend which captions go with which pictures.
● Work with the children to match the captions to the pictures. Discuss the choices made.
● Ask them to think of another caption that could be added to each picture.
● Put the children into mixed-ability pairs and give each pair an individual whiteboard and a pen.
● Display page 4 and discuss what the picture shows.
● Ask each pair to decide on a caption to add to the picture, to give some information about it. Encourage the more confident learner in the pair to write the caption on the whiteboard and hold it up for you to see.
● Share the ideas for captions and discuss the children's choices and vocabulary. Invite them to write some of the best captions on the whiteboard, with support.
● Repeat this activity, using the picture on page 5 of the Notebook file.

Independent work
● Turn the children's attention to the prepared display board (see Resources). Discuss all of the different things that are on it.
● Question the children on what they have learned about the local area during this topic work.
● In mixed-ability pairs, ask the children to choose the part of the display that they are most interested in and write a caption for it that could be added to the display
● Discuss how the work needs to be presented clearly, using a large enough text to be seen from a distance.
● Less confident learners could create their labels using ICT, using a word processor that incorporates a word bank to support their spelling and presentation.

Plenary
● Share the labels created by each pair with the rest of the class. Ask each pair to add their label to an appropriate position on the display board.
● Go to page 6 of the Notebook file and evaluate whether the labels are clear to the reader.
● Praise what is successful and make constructive suggestions for improvements where they could be made.

Whiteboard tools
Use a Pen from the Pen tray or the On-screen Keyboard, accessed through the Pen tray or the SMART Board tools menu, to write or type captions.

 Pen tray

 On-screen Keyboard

 Select tool

Making a list

Learning objective
PNS: Creating and shaping texts
● Convey information and ideas in simple non-narrative forms.

Resources
'Making a fruit kebab' Notebook file; photocopiable page 44 'How to make a fruit kebab', one for each child; different fruits as listed on page 2 of Notebook file (**NB:** Check for food allergies first!); kebab sticks; safe knives for children; sharp knife for teacher or adult assistant.

Links to other subjects
Design and technology
QCA Unit 1C 'Eat more fruit and vegetables'
● Link the work in this lesson to work on why it is important for our health to eat more fruit and vegetables.
Art and design
QCA Unit 2B 'Mother Nature, designer'
● Encourage the children to make drawings of the different fruits to use as a basis for their work in this unit.

Starter
Look at a selection of real fruits and name them. Open page 2 of the Notebook file and relate each real fruit to its picture. Read the fruit name labels, then challenge the children to add the correct label to each fruit by dragging and dropping the words at the foot of the page. Explain that they are going to use the real fruit to make a fruit kebab but that they must plan it first.

Whole-class shared work
● Let the children taste a piece of banana (be aware of any allergies that they may have). Encourage them to describe the taste of the fruit, using words such as *sweet, soft, smooth* and so on.
● Use a Pen from the Pen tray to write a list of some of the describing words on page 3.
● Repeat this with the orange.
● Discuss how the lists are set out down the page, with each new describing word on a new line. Point out that the lists are not written in sentences.
● Comment that a list would be really useful when planning the fruit kebab, to record which fruit the children want to use.
● Use page 4 to demonstrate how to make a list of fruit. Use the word bank to support spelling.
● Stress that instructions are not always given using words. On page 5, demonstrate how to create a diagram of the kebab by dragging and dropping the fruit images onto the kebab stick.
● Suggest that the children might want to consider how the finished kebab will look when making the list. Ask: *What colours and tastes will be good together? Will the fruit make a pattern?* Interchange between pages 4 and 5 to support this.

Independent work
● Give out copies of photocopiable page 44 for the children to complete. Explain that they need to complete the list of fruit and then create a labelled diagram of the kebab.
● Supply a word bank of the fruit names to support spelling if necessary.
● Provide less confident learners with more words to help them with this task.
● Adapt the sheet for more confident learners by removing the instructions at the bottom, so that they can write their own.

Plenary
● Look at page 6 of the Notebook file. Read the instructions at the bottom of the page together. Ask the children to order the instructions by pressing on each sentence at the foot of the page and dragging and dropping it into the correct position in the box above. Talk about how the instructions are set out in order, using numbers and beginning with 'bossy' words.
● Support the children as they follow their own instruction sheet to create their own fruit kebab. Chop harder fruits with the sharp knife if necessary.
● Each child can ask a friend to evaluate their kebab by looking at and tasting it. Create a list of some of the comments made in the evaluation on page 7 of the Notebook file.

Whiteboard tools
Use a Pen from the Pen tray to write and annotate on the page.

 Pen tray

 Select tool

 On-Screen Keyboard

Learning objective
PNS: Creating and shaping texts
● Create short simple texts on paper and on screen that combine words with images.

Resources
'The birthday party' Notebook file; digital camera. Make a zigzag book for each child using the instructions on photocopiable page 45 'How to make a zigzag book'.

Links to other subjects
Art and design
QCA Unit 2A 'Picture this!'
● The work on this lesson could be linked to this objective, exploring a birthday party using a variety of materials, including photography.
Speaking and listening
Objective 4: To explore familiar themes and characters through improvisation and role play.
● Ask the children to create a short role play of the story of Andrew's birthday.

Whiteboard tools
Add digital images to the page by selecting Insert, then Picture File, and browsing to where you have saved the images.

 Pen tray

 Select tool

 On-screen Keyboard

Making a picture book

Starter
In pairs, ask the children to discuss a past birthday party. Go to page 2 of the Notebook file and press the image to open the story 'Andrew's Birthday Party'. Explain that this is an interactive book and that the arrows make the pages turn. Read the title and the author's name and talk about what an author is. Read the story, discussing in detail what is happening on each page.

Whole-class shared work
● Go to page 3 of the Notebook file and use it to establish the main events in the story. Invite the children to re-order the pictures by dragging and dropping them into the correct positions on the page. Ask them to retell the story in their own words.
● Now tell the children they are going to use a drama technique called 'freeze framing' to create some digital photographs of the main events of the story. Explain that these photographs will be used to create a class book.
● Decide on the main points of the story to freeze-frame and separate the children into groups.
● Each group should create a still tableau illustrating one of the main parts of the story, and record it with a digital camera.
● Print out the digital photographs and ask the children to order them correctly. Using the children's work as a guide, insert the digital photographs into pages 4 to 11 of the Notebook file.
● Show the new book with the freeze-frame photographs and help the children retell the story in their own words. Write their ideas in the spaces provided below the photographs.

Independent work
● Give each child a blank zigzag book (see Resources). Explain that they are going to retell the story of the birthday party in their own words and pictures.
● Recap on the main points of the story and discuss what should be on the front cover.
● The children should illustrate each main point of the story on a new page of the zigzag book. Encourage them to add a simple sentence or label underneath each picture.
● Support less confident learners by giving them the digital photographs to order and stick into their zigzag books, as the illustrations. Scribe their sentences for them if necessary.
● Encourage more confident learners to add more detail to their stories.

Plenary
● Go to page 12 and share some of the books with the class. Together, evaluate the retelling and the illustrations. Highlight good use of sentences, full stops and capital letters. Make notes on the board.
● Place the finished story books in the class book corner for everyone to enjoy.
● Run the lesson over two sessions if necessary: read the story and produce the freeze-frame pictures in the first session; add the sentences to the children's pictures and create the individual zigzag books in the second session.

Learning objectives
PNS: Word recognition
PNS: Word structure and spelling

Resources
'Initial consonant clusters' Notebook file; photocopiable page 46 '+r consonant clusters', one for each child; scissors and glue; workbooks and pencils; a fan for each child made of seven narrow cards, each showing a consonant cluster (br, cr, dr, fr, gr, pr, tr), and fastened together with a split pin.

Links to other subjects
Science
QCA Unit 1C 'Sorting and using materials'
ICT
QCA Unit 1D 'Labelling and classifying'
● Extend the idea of sorting to work in science (sorting everyday objects into glass, wood, fabric and so on), and mathematics (sorting shapes or money). Present the information using a word processor with a word bank.

Whiteboard tools
Use a Highlighter pen to draw the children's attention to the consonant clusters.

 Pen tray

 Select tool

 Highlighter pen

Initial consonant clusters (1)

Starter
Open page 2 of the Notebook file. Demonstrate how to blend the two phonemes *b* and *r* together to make the *br* sound. Press the button to listen to the cluster being spoken. Tell the children that these two letters together are called a *consonant cluster*.

Repeat the activity on pages 3 to 8. Encourage the children to think of words beginning with the same consonant cluster. Use the pictures on each page to get them started with this.

Whole-class shared work
● Give each child a consonant cluster fan (see Resources) and explain how to use it to show a consonant cluster. Ask them to show specific sounds to ensure their knowledge of the spelling of the sounds is secure.
● Go to page 9 and ask the children to say what the picture shows. Repeat the word clearly.
● Encourage them to decide for themselves which consonant cluster the word begins with and to hold up that sound on their fan.
● Assess the children's answers, then ask one child to press the correct cluster from the board. A cheer will be heard when the correct answer is pressed. Show the initial consonant cluster by using the Eraser from the Pen tray to reveal the missing letters.
● Blend the whole word together to check the answer. For example, *br – i – ck → brick*.
● Repeat this activity on pages 10 to 18.

Independent work
● Provide each child with a copy of photocopiable page 46. Ask the children to cut out each word individually.
● Invite them to read each word by blending the sounds together.
● Tell them to sort the words into two piles as they read them – 'real words' and 'not real words'. They should then stick the real words into their books.
● Below each word, encourage the children to write a simple sentence containing the word.
● Give less confident learners the real words only, to sort by their initial consonant cluster to aid discrimination skills. After sorting the words, support the children in blending the sounds to read them.
● Extend more confident learners by asking them to think of their own words beginning with a given consonant cluster.

Plenary
● Work through the words on the sheet and identify whether each word was a real word or not. Encourage the children to assess their own success in this task.
● Go to page 19 of the Notebook file. Press on the top word *(brid)* and ask the children if it is a real word or not. Following their decision, invite a volunteer to drag and drop the word into the correct column on the page.
● Repeat the activity for the rest of the words on the page. Ask individual children to blend the words and sort them, assessing the learning that has taken place in the lesson.

Initial consonant clusters (2)

Starter

Open page 20 of the Notebook file. Demonstrate how to blend the two phonemes *s* and *l* together to make the *sl* sound. Press the button to listen to the cluster being spoken. Tell the children that these two letters together are called a *consonant cluster*.

Repeat the activity on pages 21 to 25. Encourage the children to think of words beginning with the same consonant cluster. Use the pictures on each page to get them started with this.

Whole-class shared work

● Give each child a consonant cluster fan (see Resources) and explain how to use it to show a consonant cluster. Ask them to show specific sounds to ensure their knowledge of the spelling of the sounds is secure.
● Display page 26 of the Notebook file. Ask the children to identify what the picture shows. Repeat the word clearly.
● Encourage them to decide for themselves which consonant cluster the word begins with and to hold up that sound on their fans.
● Assess the children's answers, then invite one child to drag two letters from the bottom of the page onto the line at the beginning of the word to make the correct cluster.
● Use the Delete button ☒ to delete the box concealing the word to check the answer.
● Finally, blend the whole word together to check the answer. For example, *sl – u – g → slug*.
● Repeat this activity on pages 27 to 31.

Independent work

● Give out copies of photocopiable page 47. Explain to the children that they must make pairs of socks by matching the consonant cluster onset to the rime, to make a real word.
● Invite them to write the words they make in their workbooks.
● Below each word, encourage them to write a simple sentence containing the word.
● Less confident learners could match socks that have been cut out and laminated. The socks could be colour-coded to aid the matching process. After making the words, help the children to blend the onset and rime to read them.
● Extend more confident learners by asking them to think of different ways of pairing the socks (for example, *clip, clan, blob, blot*), and to make their own words beginning with a given consonant cluster.

Plenary

● Use the enlarged and laminated socks to share the answers to the work done on the sheet. Ask the children to choose two socks that make a word and hold them up together. Encourage them to assess their own success in this task.
● Display page 32 of the Notebook file. Read the onsets and rimes on the page. Ask individual children to match the onsets to the rimes to make a real word.
● Assess the learning that has taken place in the lesson.

Final consonant clusters

Learning objectives
PNS: Word recognition
PNS: Word structure and spelling

Resources
'Final consonant clusters' Notebook file; for each group of three, an A3 copy of photocopiable page 48 'Final consonant cluster bingo', cut into boards and individual cards; counters; bingo instructions (available on the CD); for each child, a fan made of six narrow cards, each showing a consonant cluster (st, sp, sk, nd, nt, nk), and fastened together with a split pin.

Links to other subjects
Speaking and listening
Objective 2: To listen with sustained concentration.
● Encourage the children to listen carefully to the ends of the words.
Science
QCA Unit 1C 'Sorting and using materials'
● Extend the idea of dressing Fred by discussing how we dress for different types of weather, and how the materials of the clothes we choose reflect this.

Whiteboard tools
Use a Highlighter pen to highlight consonant clusters in the Plenary.

 Pen tray

 Select tool

 Highlighter pen

Starter
Open page 2 of the Notebook file. Demonstrate how to blend the two phonemes *s* and *t* together to make the *st* sound. Ask the children to blend the sounds together on pages 3 to 7. Press the button on each page to listen to the cluster being spoken. Tell the children that these two letters together are called *consonant clusters*. Explain that consonant clusters can be at the end of a word as well as at the beginning of it. Ask them to think of words ending with each of the clusters.

Whole-class shared work
● Give each child a consonant cluster fan (see Resources) and explain how to use it to show a consonant cluster. Ask the children to show specific sounds to ensure their knowledge of the spelling of the sounds is secure.
● Look at page 8 of the Notebook file and read the words at the bottom of the page together.
● Ask a child to choose one of the words and read it aloud. Invite the rest of the class to show which consonant cluster the word ends with by holding up the appropriate cluster on their fans.
● Sort all of the words by dragging and dropping them into the correct group on the Notebook page.
● Repeat this activity on page 9.
● Use page 10 to assess the children's ability to read words with final consonant clusters. Ask them to read the word on the top card. Encourage them to use their new knowledge of final consonant clusters to try to blend the words. If they read the word correctly, allow one child to add an item of clothing to Fred and then put the card into the bin.
● Continue to read the cards until Fred is completely dressed.

Independent work
● Put the children into similar ability groups of three. Give each group two bingo boards and a set of word cards created from photocopiable page 48, plus some counters.
● Go to page 11 of the Notebook file and explain the rules of the game to the children.
● Ensure the caller checks the other players' choices and corrects them if necessary.
● Support less confident learners with reading the word cards and show the cards to the players to help them find the correct final cluster if necessary.
● Encourage more confident learners to think of other words ending in these consonant clusters.

Plenary
● Go to page 12 of the Notebook file. Ask the children to read the words on the cards at the bottom of the page and highlight the consonant clusters in each of them.
● Tell the children that these words are answers to the clues above. Ask them to read out each clue and then work as a class to match the answer cards to them. Invite volunteers to drag and drop the words into the appropriate spaces next to the clues.
● Repeat this activity on page 13.

Spelling high frequency words

Learning objective
PNS: Word structure and spelling

Resources
'High frequency words' Notebook file; individual whiteboards and pens; each child needs a 'look-cover-write-check' sheet suitable for their level of ability: list five words down the side of the page, then add three more short lines after each word across the page (see page 20 of the Notebook file for a reference); strips of card to cover words on the sheet.

Links to other subjects
Encourage the children to learn to spell topic words in history, geography, science and mathematics (for example, shapes), using the 'look-cover-write-check' method.

Whiteboard tools
Use the On-screen Keyboard, accessed through the Pen tray or the SMART Board tools menu, to alter words as necessary.

 Pen tray

 Select tool

 On-screen Keyboard

 Screen Shade

Starter
Display page 19 of the Notebook file. Explain that the groups of letters are anagrams of colour words and that the colour of the letters gives a clue to what the words should say. Challenge the children to re-order the letters so that each colour word is spelled correctly.

Whole-class shared work
- Go to page 20 of the Notebook file. If you need to alter the words so that they are appropriate for the needs of your children, double-press on the word and use the On-screen Keyboard to type in a different word.
- Provide the children with individual whiteboards and pens.
- Explain the process of learning spellings using the look–cover–write–check method.
- Tell the children to look closely at the first word, thinking about its shape, length and any familiar letter patterns.
- Move the cover over the word and ask the children to write it on their individual whiteboards.
- Invite a volunteer to write the word in the white box on the Notebook page.
- Uncover the word and encourage the children to check their spelling against it.
- Repeat for the other four words on the page.
- Pages 21 to 25 offer word-tracking activities to help focus children on the letter order in each of the words. (Change the words and letters to match the words used on page 20 if you have altered these already.)
- Ask a child to track along the row of letters from left to right and drag the correct letters into the box at the bottom of the page as they reach them, to build the word.

Independent work
- Give each child a prepared sheet of words and a strip of card (see Resources). Say that they have ten minutes to look at each word carefully, cover it up with the strip of card, write it and then check it.
- Tell the children not to look at the words while they write them. They should practise each word three times using the lines provided.
- Stress that look-cover-write-check is a good strategy for learning new spellings.
- The words used should be differentiated for less confident and more confident learners.
- As an extension, create practical word-tracking activities using plastic letters or cards with letters on them. Alternatively, create these on paper and ask the children to draw a ring around each letter they need, in order from left to right.

Plenary
- Use page 26 of the Notebook file to give the children a spelling test. Ask them to spell the five words that they learned on page 20. Use the Screen Shade to hide the words. Then invite the children to swap their work with a friend and check against the board.
- Once they have completed this, test each group on the spelling of the five words they learned during their independent work.

Plurals

Starter
Open the Notebook file and look at the pictures on page 2. Identify what each picture shows. Point to one picture at a time and challenge the children to write the name of the object on an individual whiteboard. Ask one child to write the word beneath the picture on the whiteboard. Correct any spelling mistakes as necessary.

Whole-class shared work
● Ask the children what they would call more than one girl. Elicit the answer 'girls'. Ask: *How has the word changed?*
● Open page 3 of the Notebook file and go through it with the children. Expain the term *plural*. Use the Delete button ☒ to delete the star to reveal the answer. Point out that an *s* is added to many words to make them plural.
● Show the children page 4 and point out that they are the same pictures as on page 2, but now there are more than one of each of the objects.
● Again using individual whiteboards, invite the children to write down what each picture is. Remind them that the words should now be plural.
● More confident learners could attempt to write the number word, to show how many there are of each object.
● Ask different children to write each word beneath the picture. Point out the words are spelled the same as before except that an *s* has been added to the end to make it plural.

Independent work
● Give each group a set of prepared cards and a word bank (see Resources).
● Talk with the children about what is on each card. Explain that the names of the objects are in the word bank to help them spell the words more easily.
● Ask the children to write down exactly what they can see on the card in their books (for example: *5 cakes*). Remind them again that there is more than one of each object, so the word must be made plural.
● Work with less confident learners in a group, until they understand the concept of adding *s*.
● To extend the activity, challenge more confident learners to put the words into a sentence. For example: *She had 5 cakes for tea.*

Plenary
● Put the children into pairs. Display page 5 of the Notebook file and ask the children to read the words with their partner. Look at each word individually and ask the children to make it plural. Invite them to add *s* to the end of the words to make the spelling correct.
● Challenge each pair to choose one of the plural words, put it into a sentence and write the sentence on an individual whiteboard.
● Invite one pair to write their sentence on page 5. Highlight the use of the *s* on the end of the word to make it plural.

Missing words

Learning objective
PNS: Understanding and
interpreting texts
● Use syntax and context
when reading for meaning.

Resources
'Missing words' Notebook file;
Big Book with a few words
covered with sticky notes;
individual whiteboards and
pens. Before the lesson, write
simple sentences with a word
missing from them onto
individual cards.

Links to other subjects
Citizenship
QCA Unit 2 'Choices'
● Use the Goldilocks story as
a basis for a discussion on
right and wrong behaviour.
Use this as an opportunity to
discuss personal choices and
decisions, and how these
affect the people around us.

Starter

With the children, discuss different strategies that can be used to decode unfamiliar words. Remind them particularly of using the text in the rest of the sentence to work out a word. Explain that it is often helpful to re-read the sentence again, or read the rest of the sentence and then go back and try to fill in the missing word.

Read the Big Book (see Resources) and use the strategies discussed to guess what the covered words might be.

Whole-class shared work

● Open page 2 of the Notebook file. Tell the children that some words are missing from the sentences. You would like them to work out what the missing words are.
● Ask them to explain how they could work out each missing word. Refer them back to the strategies discussed in the Starter.
● Invite a child to read the first sentence, leaving a gap for the missing word.
● Provide each pair with an individual whiteboard and a pen. Ask them to write down their idea of what the missing word is.
● Listen to some of the children's ideas and try them in the sentence. Discuss which words work, and which do not.
● Use the Eraser from the Pen tray to rub over the empty spaces in each sentence to reveal what the missing word actually is.
● Repeat this for all of the sentences on pages 2 and 3 of the Notebook file.

Independent work

● Give out a set of prepared sentence cards to each group (see Resources).
● Tell the children to read the sentences on the cards and discuss what the missing words could be with a talking partner in their group. Suggest they try the words decided upon in the sentences to see if they make sense.
● Ask them to write the sentences in their workbooks with the missing words included.
● Support less confident learners by giving them a choice of two words to put into the gap. Ask them to decide which of the two words makes sense in the sentence.
● Encourage more confident learners to make up their own 'missing word' sentences, to try on each other.

Plenary

● Go to page 4 of the Notebook file. Discuss some of the sentences the children have investigated.
● Listen to some of the ideas that the children had about what the missing words could be. Discuss which of the ideas would work and which would not, and explain why. Make notes on the board.

Whiteboard tools
Use the Eraser to reveal the
missing words in the whole-
class activity. Use a Pen from
the Pen tray to make notes on
the board.

 Pen tray

 Select tool

Full stops

Learning objective
PNS: Sentence structure and punctuation
● Use capital letters and full stops when punctuating simple sentences.

Resources
'Punctuation' Notebook file; Big Book; workbooks and pencils. Before the lesson, prepare a set cards for each group, each card showing two simple, related sentences with the full stops omitted (ensure that the sentences don't always end at the end of a line).

Links to other subjects
Encourage the children to use sentences with capital letters and full stops in their writing for topics in history, geography and science, as well as English.

Starter
Introduce the punctuation game to the children. Tell them that they are going to read a Big Book story aloud, and when they see a capital letter or full stop they are going to do an action. For a capital letter, they must put both hands straight up in the air to make themselves tall like a capital letter. For a full stop, they must stab the air with their index fingers as though they are making a full stop. Read the Big Book story aloud together slowly, and add the actions.

Whole-class shared work
● Ask: *Where do we find full stops?*
● Go to page 6 of the Notebook file. Explain that full stops are found at the end of a sentence and are followed by a capital letter, if another sentence follows on.
● Read the sentences on page 7 together. Ask: *Why are these sentences?* (They begin with a capital letter, end with a full stop and make sense on their own.)
● Encourage the children to look closely at the sentences to find the full stops. Invite them to use a Highlighter pen to highlight them. Point out that the full stop is always at the end of the sentence.
● Display page 8. Ask the children to identify what is wrong. Invite volunteers to come to the whiteboard to add the missing full stops. After all the full stops have been added, suggest that a child pulls the screen from the left-hand side of the page across the text to check the answers.
● Look at some sentences in the Big Book. Find examples where the sentence runs onto the next line of text. Point out that the full stops are always at the end of a sentence, but not always at the end of a line. Make this difference very clear.

Independent work
● Give each group a set of prepared cards (see Resources).
● Tell the children to choose a card and re-write it in their workbooks, with the full stops in the correct place.
● Stop the children at various points and ask them to check what they have done so far to make sure that each sentence ends with a full stop.
● Give less confident learners cards with one sentence, so that they only have to add the full stop to the end.
● Challenge more confident learners to write their own sentences about a given topic, using full stops where appropriate.

Plenary
● Look at some of the work completed by the children and comment on what they have done well. Rectify any common mistakes.
● Look at page 9 and work as a class to decide where to put the full stops in the passage. Add the full stops by either using the On-screen Keyboard to type them in, or using a Pen from the Pen tray to write them.
● Keep re-reading the text, pausing at the full stops already placed, to help the children to check their decisions.

Whiteboard tools
Use a Highlighter pen to highlight full stops in the text.

 Pen tray

 Select tool

 Highlighter pen

 On-screen Keyboard

Design a superhero

Starter
Hand out a superhero comic book to each pair of children. Give them a few minutes to look at it together, then ask different pairs to tell the rest of the class a little bit about the superhero in their comic.

Go to page 2 of the Notebook file and ask the children to suggest a superhero. Discuss what the superhero is like, asking questions such as: *What is his/her name? What does he/she look like? What are his/her powers? Who is he/she in 'real' life?* Repeat with other superheroes.

Whole-class shared work
● Ask the children to look carefully at the superhero characters on page 3 of the Notebook file. Point out that they won't have seen these characters in a comic – they are 'new' superheroes.
● Read the descriptive sentences at the bottom of the page and tell the children that each sentence describes one of the two characters.
● Invite the children to discuss with a partner which sentences describe which character. Then ask volunteers to come to the whiteboard to drag the sentences into the correct boxes.
● Challenge the children to think of other descriptive sentences about each character.
● Go to page 4 of the Notebook file. Explain to the children that they are going to write a character profile of a superhero. Ask them to decide upon a superhero and write the name on the line provided. Ask a volunteer to come up and draw the superhero in the box.
● Explain what each of the headings requires. For example, suggest that for 'Heroic actions' the children could write about a time when the character saved the world.
● Encourage them to identify sensible phrases and sentences for each heading.
● Look closely at vocabulary choices. Invite the children to improve their ideas where possible by altering or adding words.

Independent work
● Provide each child with a copy of photocopiable page 49.
● Ask the children to invent their own superhero. They should first draw a picture of their 'new' superhero on the photocopiable sheet and then complete a written description of him/her.
● Encourage the children to consider their vocabulary choices carefully, and choose interesting and accurate describing words.
● Supply a word bank of useful words to support less confident learners.
● Extend more confident learners by asking them to write their description, using their own sentences, in a short passage.

Plenary
● Go to page 5 of the Notebook file. Invite the children to share some of their superheroes with the rest of the class.
● Evaluate the vocabulary choices made and discuss whether more detail could have been added to the description.
● Encourage the rest of the class to ask the inventor questions about their superhero that they must answer. Make notes on the board as appropriate.

Retelling a story

Learning objectives
PNS: Speaking
● Retell stories, ordering events using story language.
PNS: Text structure and organisation
● Write chronological texts using simple structures.

Resources
'The Three Little Sheep' Notebook file; tape recorder and microphone; paper and pencils; pre-cut card arrows.

Links to other subjects
Design and technology
QCA Unit 1D 'Homes'
Art and design
QCA Unit 2C 'Can buildings speak?'
● Construct models or create pictures of different buildings used as homes.
Speaking and listening
Objective 8: To act out well-known stories.
● Act out the story of 'The Three Little Pigs'.

Whiteboard tools
If a microphone is available, use Windows® Sound Recorder (accessed through Start> Programs>Accessories> Entertainment) to record the children's stories. Attach the sound files to the page by selecting Insert, then Sound, and browsing to where you have saved the files.

 Pen tray

 Select tool

 On-Screen Keyboard

 Blank Page button

Starter
Open page 2 of the Notebook file. Press the thumbnail image to go to the electronic storybook 'The Three Little Sheep'. Read the story with the children. Discuss different ways to decipher unfamiliar words and encourage the children to use these strategies to help them read the text. Talk about what is happening in the story and clarify the main events. Ask: *Does it remind you of another story?* Compare the story to 'The Three Little Pigs', making notes on the board.

Whole-class shared work
● Ask the children to recall the opening sentence used in the story (*Once upon a time...*). Work with the children to list alternative ways of starting this story.
● Display page 3 and ask the children to look carefully at the illustrations.
● Invite them to work as a team to re-arrange the illustrations so that they tell the story in the correct order.
● Suggest that they could add a short caption to each illustration to help retell the story in more detail. Ask them to choose an illustration and think of a caption to accompany it.
● Go to page 4. Invite the children to retell the story orally to a talking partner. Encourage the listening partner to add any omitted details as they listen.
● Using pages 5 to 15, invite individual children to use the On-screen Keyboard to type a caption next to each picture to add more detail to the pictorial retelling.
● Share the newly created text as a class and discuss how it could be improved even further.

Independent work
● Look at the correctly ordered illustrations on page 3 of the Notebook file. Remind the children that they illustrate the main parts of the story. State what these main parts are.
● Split the children into groups of ten and assign one main part of the story to each group member.
● Invite the children to create an illustration for their part of the story and then ask them think of a caption to accompany it. They should write the caption on a strip of paper and attach it to the illustration.
● The group members should then bring their work together and arrange it into the correct sequence to retell the story. Supply each group with pre-cut card arrows to help them organise their work.
● Give each group access to a tape recorder and ask them to record an oral retelling of their story. Suggest that each child retells his or her own part of the story in sequence. State that it is probable that they will put more detail into their oral retelling than they did into their caption. (Windows® Sound Recorder can be used as an alternative to a tape recorder.)

Plenary
● Go to page 16. Scan each group's work and then place each child's illustration on a new Notebook page in the correct order. (Use the Blank Page button to add extra pages to the Notebook file.)
● Share each group's work with the class by playing back the tape recording and moving to the relevant pages in the Notebook file as needed.
● Invite the children to evaluate each group's retelling of the story.

Labelling body parts

Learning objectives
PNS: Creating and shaping texts
● Convey information and ideas in simple non-narrative forms.
● Find and use new and interesting words.

Resources
'Labels and captions' Notebook file; Big Book about the human body; drawing paper and pencils.

Links to other subjects
Science
QCA Unit 1A 'Ourselves'
● Link the work in this lesson to the above objective.
Art and design
QCA Unit 1A 'Self-portrait'
● Extend the activity in the Plenary to further discussion about faces and expressions, and link this to making a self-portrait.

Starter
Introduce the Big Book to the children. Decide whether the text is fiction or non-fiction, and identify reasons why. Point out the title and author of the book on the front cover. Look at the contents page (if there is one) and discuss what it is for and how to use it. Read a few pages of the book and discuss what the children have learned from them. Look particularly closely at any labelled drawings or diagrams and discuss what they show and how they show it.

Whole-class shared work
● Tell the children that they are going to practise reading and writing labels for drawings and diagrams.
● Go to page 7 of the Notebook file and share the labelled diagram of the parts of the body with the children.
● Invite different children to read the labels. Show how the arrows are used to point to that part of the body.
● To ensure the children are really comfortable with the words, ask different children to highlight specific words as you say them.
● Go to page 8 and explain that the children now need to match the correct labels to the body parts. Encourage them to look where an arrow is pointing, then find that word in the list on the left-hand side of the page and drag it into place.
● Correct any errors or misconceptions as necessary.

Independent work
● Display page 9 of the Notebook file. Tell the children to refer to it for reference when necessary.
● Give each child a plain piece of paper and ask them to draw a detailed picture of a full person.
● Next, ask them to add labels to their drawings to show the names of the different body parts.
● Give less confident learners a ready-drawn body with arrows pointing to the body parts they need to label. Supply a word bank for the names of the body parts where necessary.
● Challenge more confident learners to label some other parts of the body (for example, toes).

Plenary
● Show some of the children's labelling work to the class and evaluate the effectiveness of their labelling. Ask: *Is it clear which part of the body each label points to? Are the labels written clearly?*
● Display page 10 of the Notebook file. Ask the children to work with a partner to decide what label would be appropriate for each part of the face.
● Invite different children to come to the whiteboard and use a Pen from the Pen tray to label the parts of the face.

Whiteboard tools
Use a Highlighter pen to highlight vocabulary relating to the human body. Use a Pen from the Pen tray to label the face in the Plenary.

 Pen tray

 Select tool

 Highlighter pen

Describing old toys

Learning objectives
PNS: Creating and shaping texts
● Convey information and ideas in simple non-narrative forms.
● Find and use new and interesting words and phrases, including story language.
● Create short simple texts on paper that combine words with images.
PNS: Sentence structure and punctuation
● Compose and write simple sentences independently to communicate meaning.

Resources
'Describing old toys' Notebook file; photocopiable page 50 'Describing old toys', one for each child; a collection of old toys to be examined and handled by the children.

Links to other subjects
History
QCA Unit 1 'How are our toys different from those in the past?'
Science
QCA Unit 1C 'Sorting and using materials'
ICT
QCA Unit 1D 'Labelling and classifying'
● All the above objectives link well to this lesson.

Whiteboard tools
Use the Shapes tool to cover the pictures in the Plenary. Insert scanned images by selecting Insert, then Picture File, and browsing to where you have saved the images.

 Pen tray

 Select tool

 On-Screen Keyboard

 Shapes tool

Starter
Make a museum display of the old toys. Choose one toy and let the children have a close look at it.

Go to page 2 of the Notebook file. Invite pairs to spend one minute talking about the toy. Ask them to consider what it is, what it does, what it looks like and what it is made from. Bring the class together to share some of their ideas. Record some of the ideas on the Notebook page.

Whole-class shared work
● Explain that museums catalogue their artefacts so that they have a written record of everything they own.
● Tell the children that they are going to create a catalogue of the toys in the class museum.
● Use pages 3 to 6 to explore some catalogue descriptions of old toys. Read and discuss the phrases. Stress that they give information as a list, using bullet points.
● Invite the children to write a descriptive sentence about the toy at the bottom of the page. They could use one of the phrases as a basis for the sentence, or invent a completely new sentence.
● Use page 7 to practise writing descriptive phrases that give information about a toy. Look closely at the picture and discuss what it is, what it does, what it looks like and what it is made from.
● List some descriptive phrases next to the bullet points. Challenge the children to write a simple descriptive sentence about the toy on the line at the bottom of the page.

Independent work
● Give each group of children a few different toys to examine. Allow enough time for the groups to look carefully at the toys and discuss them.
● Give out copies of photocopiable page 50. Ask each child to choose a toy to catalogue. They should draw a labelled picture and list some descriptive phrases about it.
● Encourage the children to make good vocabulary choices that give clear information about the toy.
● Offer a word bank for less confident learners to help them access technical vocabulary.
● As an extension, challenge more confident learners to turn their phrases into a short passage describing the toy.

Plenary
● Set out the toys that have been described so that the whole class can see them. Scan some of the catalogue descriptions onto page 8, covering the pictures using the Shapes tool .
● Show each description and challenge the children to identify which toy is being described. Ask: *How did you know it was this toy? What could be changed or added to make it clearer which toy is being described?*
● Work with the children to turn one of the lists into a short passage, using capital letters and full stops correctly.

Long vowel phoneme *ee*

Learning objective
PNS: Word recognition
● Recognise/use alternative ways of spelling the phonemes already taught (eg /ae/ sound spelled with 'ai', 'ay' or 'a-e'; /ee/ sound spelled as 'ea' and 'e').

Resources
'Long vowel phonemes' Notebook file; photocopiable page 51 'Long vowel graphemes *ee* or *ea*', one for each child; Big Book that demonstrates the long vowel phoneme *ee*; individual whiteboards and pens.

Links to other subjects
ICT
QCA Unit 1C 'The information around us'
● Ask the children to create an *ee/ea* word book or poster, combining pictures and words.

Starter
Introduce the long vowel phoneme *ee*. Go to page 2 of the Notebook file, show the children the different graphemes (*ee* and *ea*) for the *ee* phoneme, and demonstrate the sound it makes in words.

Read the Big Book as a class. Ask the children to indicate every time they hear a word containing the *ee* phoneme. Write some of the words on page 2 and highlight the grapheme that is responsible for the sound.

Whole-class shared work
● Go to page 3. Ask individual children to read the words on the page and point out that all of the words contain the *ee* phoneme spelled using the *ee* grapheme.
● Now look at page 4 in the same way but this time point out that all of the words contain the *ee* phoneme spelled using the *ea* grapheme.
● Challenge the children to think of other words containing the *ee* phoneme that were not on the two pages.
● Read the sentences on page 5 and identify the words that contain the *ee* phoneme. Ask individual children to highlight these words and identify which grapheme each contains.
● Show the children page 6 of the Notebook file. Ask them to name the picture, decide which spelling is correct and to write it on their individual whiteboards.
● After they have done this, use the Delete button ⊠ (or select the Delete option from the dropdown menu) to remove the blue rectangle to check the answer.
● Repeat this activity on pages 7 to 10, to identify children who need more support.

Independent work
● Provide each child with a copy of photocopiable page 51. Discuss what each picture shows. Remind the children that each word contains an *ee* sound.
● Ask the children to complete the spellings by adding the correct grapheme – *ee* or *ea*.
● Show more confident learners how to use a dictionary to check words that they are unsure how to spell. Allow them to support the less confident learners in finding the words.
● Then read the sentences together, and ensure everyone knows what the words with the missing graphemes are.
● Ask the children to fill in the missing graphemes in the sentences, encouraging them to check their spellings using a simple dictionary.

Plenary
● The children should check their answers with a friend from a different table, discussing any answers that are different. Support the children in resolving disagreements by showing them how to check the words in a simple dictionary.
● Show the class page 11 of the Notebook file and ask them to identify the sound that *ee* and *ea* make. Give out individual whiteboards and ask the children to write down four words containing the *ee* phoneme. List these on the board.

Whiteboard tools
Use a Pen from the Pen tray to write words on the board. Use a Highlighter pen to highlight parts of the words.

 Pen tray

 Highlighter pen

 Select tool

 Delete button

Long vowel phoneme *oa*

Learning objective
PNS: Word recognition
● Recognise/use alternative ways of spelling the phonemes already taught (eg /ae/ sound spelled with 'ai', 'ay' or 'a-e'; /ee/ sound spelled as 'ea' and 'e').

Resources
'Long vowel phonemes' Notebook file; photocopiable page 52 'Long vowel graphemes *oa* or *ow*', one for each child; Big Book that demonstrates the long vowel phoneme *oa*; individual whiteboards and pens.

Links to other subjects
ICT
QCA Unit 1C 'The information around us'
● Ask the children to extend their *ee/ea* word book (see Lesson 22) by adding an *oa/ow* section. Alternatively, they can continue their series of long vowel phoneme posters, by creating an *oa/ow* poster, combining pictures and words.

Starter
Go to page 12 of the Notebook file. Introduce the long vowel phoneme *oa*. Show the children the different graphemes (*oa* and *ow*) for the phoneme and demonstrate the sound it makes in words.

Read the Big Book as a class. Ask the children to indicate every time they hear a word containing the *oa* phoneme. Write some of the words on page 12 and highlight the grapheme in each word that is responsible for the sound.

Whole-class shared work
● Go to page 13 and ask the children to read the two graphemes. Note that they make the same sound even though they are spelled differently.
● Challenge the children to think of words containing the *oa* phoneme and write them on page 13.
● Read the words on the cards on page 14 of the Notebook file. Encourage the children to sort the words into the correct columns, then read each list together.
● Ask a child to press the sound icons on page 15 and tell the class to listen carefully to the words.
● Invite the children to write on their individual whiteboards the words they hear, considering the spelling carefully. Check the words as a class.
● Go to page 16 and ask the children to decide, in pairs, which answer goes with which clue.
● Drag the answers to the side of each clue and then use the Fill Colour tool 🔳 to change the red boxes to white to check them.

Independent work
● Give out copies of photocopiable page 52 and put the children into mixed-ability pairs.
● Ensure that all the children understand how to complete a crossword. Encourage the more confident learner in each pair to support the less able with filling in the answers correctly.
● Ask the children to read the clues in their pairs and work out what the answers could be. Remind them regularly that the answers to the clues all contain the *oa* phoneme.
● Tell the children to fill in the words on their own crossword sheet, ensuring that they spell them correctly.
● Support the children in using a dictionary to check any spellings of words that they are unsure about.
● As an extension, challenge the children to think of other words containing the *oa* phoneme.

Plenary
● Show the children a correctly completed crossword. Ask them to check their own answers and assess their own success.
● Use page 17 of the Notebook file to assess any children that you are still unsure about. Discuss any errors made and correct them. Finally, use the Eraser from the Pen tray to reveal the answers.

Whiteboard tools
Use a Pen from the Pen tray to write words on the board and a Highlighter pen to highlight parts of the words.

 Pen tray

 Select tool

 Highlighter pen

 Fill Colour tool

Long vowel phoneme *oo*

Learning objective
PNS: Word recognition
● Recognise/use alternative ways of spelling the phonemes already taught (eg /ae/ sound spelled with 'ai', 'ay' or 'a-e'; /ee/ sound spelled as 'ea' and 'e').

Resources
'Long vowel phonemes' Notebook file; photocopiable page 53 'Long vowel graphemes *oo, ew* or *ue*', one for each child; Big Book to demonstrate the *oo, ew, ue* graphemes. Before the lesson, make a set of three cards for each child, each card displaying a different grapheme (*oo, ew, ue*).

Links to other subjects
ICT
QCA Unit 1C 'The information around us'
● Ask the children to extend their long vowel phonemes word book (see Lessons 22 and 23) by adding an *oo/ew/ue* section. Alternatively, they can continue their series of wall posters by creating an *oo/ew/ue* poster, combining pictures and words.

Whiteboard tools
Use a Pen from the Pen tray to write words on the board. Use a Highlighter pen to highlight parts of the words.

 Pen tray

 Highlighter pen

 Select tool

Starter
Go to page 18 of the Notebook file. Introduce the long vowel phoneme *oo*. Show the children the different graphemes (*oo, ew* and *ue*) for the *oo* phoneme, and demonstrate the sound it makes in words.

Read the Big Book as a class. Ask the children to indicate every time they hear a word containing the *oo* phoneme. Write some of the words on the Notebook page, and highlight the grapheme in each word that is responsible for the sound.

Whole-class shared work
● Go to page 19 and read the words at the bottom of the page. Elicit from the children that all of the words contain the *oo* phoneme.
● Challenge the children to sort the words into the correct boxes according to the grapheme they contain.
● Read the sentences on page 20 of the Notebook file and work out together what the words with missing graphemes should say.
● Give out the set of three cards (see Resources) to each child and ask them to show the grapheme that they think is missing from each word.
● Decide as a class on the correct graphemes and drag them into place.
● Challenge the children to think of other words that contain the *oo* phoneme.
● Invite individual children to come to the whiteboard to write words containing the *oo* phoneme on page 21. Ask other children to highlight the grapheme in the word written.

Independent work
● Hand out copies of photocopiable page 53. Ask the children to read the words in the word bank at the bottom of the sheet quietly to themselves. Support less confident learners by clarifying any words they are unsure of.
● Read the sentences together and explain that each word in the word bank fits into one of the gaps in the sentences, so that the sentence makes sense.
● Encourage the children to re-read the sentences with the word fitted in, to check that they make sense.
● Reduce the number of sentences and words for less confident learners.
● As an extension, invite the children to put the words in the word bank into new sentences.

Plenary
● Make a card that clearly displays each grapheme. Stick the cards on different walls of the school hall or other large open space. Ask the children to note where each grapheme is. Tell them they must listen to the word you say and then select the grapheme it contains.
● Say a word and encourage the children to move towards the grapheme they think it contains. Repeat this with other words.
● Watch carefully for the children who follow the crowd, as these may need more input on the long vowel phoneme *oo*.

Magic e

Starter
Revise the different ways to spell each of the long vowel phonemes. Go to page 2 of the Notebook file and explain that these sounds can also be created using a split digraph. Explain that this is made using a vowel, then a consonant or consonant blend, then an *e*. When the *e* is added it tells the vowel to make a long sound instead of the short sound it would usually make. Write a few examples on the board to illustrate these points.

Sing the song on page 3, to the tune of 'This Old Man, He Played One', to help the children remember this new concept.

Whole-class shared work
● Look at page 4 and read the words. Point out that each vowel makes a short sound.
● Challenge the children to add *magic e* to the end of each word on their individual whiteboards, and investigate how the words change.
● Use the Eraser from the Pen tray to check the words created and read them aloud.
● Emphasise the change the vowel has made from a short sound to a long sound. Remind the children this has happened because of *magic e*.
● Tell the children to read and sort the words on the cards on page 5 using their *magic e* knowledge. Emphasise the long vowel sound created in each word.
● Ask the children to think of sentences containing the real words.

Independent work
● Give each group a set of prepared cards (see Resources) and a pencil.
● Ask the children to choose a card and read the word on it. Stress that the vowels in these words will make a short vowel sound as there is no *magic e* on the end of them.
● Tell the children to add *magic e* to the end of the word and read the new word created. Stress that the vowel will now make a long vowel sound because *magic e* has altered the sound it makes.
● Challenge the children to decide whether the word created is a real word or not.
● Tell them to list the words under the headings 'real words' or 'not real words'.
● Encourage them to share their lists with a talking partner and resolve any differences of opinion through discussion.
● Give less confident learners only those words containing one of the vowels.
● Extend more confident learners by asking them to put the real words created into sentences instead of just listing them.

Plenary
● Discuss and compare the words created during the independent work.
● Show page 6 of the Notebook file and ask the children to name the objects. Challenge them to spell each of the words on individual whiteboards, then ask one child to come up to the whiteboard to write the word on screen in the space provided.
● Once they have done this, use the Eraser from the Pen tray to reveal the correct answer. Assess and review the children's responses.
● Repeat the same activity on page 7.

Vowels and consonants

Learning objective
PNS: Word recognition
● Recognise automatically an increasing number of high frequency words.

Resources
Prepare a Notebook file: Page 1 - the alphabet; Page 2 - ten high frequency words; Page 3 - two boxes labelled 'vowel' and 'consonant', and a collection of high frequency words with different initial letters (vowels and consonants), as separate text boxes. Write 15 high frequency words onto cards, each with a different initial letter (vowels and consonants). You will also need coloured pencils and paper for the children.

Links to other subjects
Mathematics
PNS: Handling data
ICT
QCA Unit 1E 'Representing information graphically'
● Ask the children to sort their names into those beginning with vowels or consonants, and represent this as a pictogram on the computer. They could also sort how many names there are in the class that begin with each of the vowels.

Whiteboard tools
Create the Notebook file using a Pen from the Pen tray and the Shapes tool. Use a Highlighter pen to highlight different letters.

 Pen tray

 On-screen Keyboard

 Shapes tool

 Highlighter pen

 Select tool

Starter
Sing the alphabet song with the children to revise alphabetical order. Open page 1 of the Notebook file you have prepared (see Resources) and ask the children to read out the alphabet. Explain that there are five vowels in the alphabet and show which letters they are. State that the rest of the letters are consonants. Explain that the consonant sounds are created using the lips, tongue and teeth, unlike the vowel sounds.

Whole-class shared work
● Ask specific children to highlight the vowels in the alphabet and say the vowels together.
● Go to page 2 of your prepared Notebook file and read the high frequency words. Ask the children to put the words into sentences to confirm their meanings.
● Invite individuals to come to the whiteboard and use a Highlighter pen to highlight the vowels in a particular word. Ask them to say which letters they have highlighted.
● Go to page 3. Encourage the children to read the words shown and put them into sentences to confirm their meanings.
● Tell them to focus on the initial letter of each word, and invite them to decide whether each word begins with a vowel or a consonant.
● Ask them to sort the words into two groups according to their initial letter (vowel or consonant), using the labelled boxes on the page.

Independent work
● Challenge the children to work in pairs to write the whole alphabet in order. Tell them to write the vowels in a different colour to the rest of the letters.
● Check the children's alphabet work before continuing and correct any mistakes.
● Give each pair a set of the word cards that you prepared before the lesson (see Resources).
● Ask the children to read each of the words with a partner and clarify any they are unsure about.
● Invite the children to sort the words into two groups according to whether the word begins with a vowel or a consonant. Remind them they can refer back to their alphabet.
● Make the task easier for less confident learners by asking them to sort cards displaying single letters and not whole words.
● As an extension, ask the children to highlight all of the vowels in the words by drawing a circle around them with a light-coloured pencil.

Plenary
● Ask the class to consider the initial letter of their first name and sort themselves into two groups: those whose name begins with a vowel and those whose name begins with a consonant.
● Show some high frequency words and target individual children to read them. Ask the children to show on their fingers how many vowels there are in the words and then identify these letters.

Question marks

Starter

Display page 10 of the Notebook file. Read the sentences together, then look carefully at the initial word and the end of each sentence and ask the children what they notice. Conclude that each sentence is a question because it ends with a question mark and begins with a question word. Ask the children to highlight the question marks using one colour and the question words using another colour. Invite them to draw some question marks in the air with their fingers to practise their formation.

Whole-class shared work

- Ask the children to explain how they would identify whether a sentence was a question or a statement.
- Show the children page 11. Ask them whether the top sentence (*This jumper is blue*) is a statement or a question, and invite a volunteer to drag it into the correct box. Get the children to sort the rest of the sentences in the same way. Ask them to clarify how they know which set each sentence belongs to.
- Devise a collection of question words (for example, *what, can, how, where*) and list them on page 12.
- Challenge the children to think of an example question that begins with each word.
- Introduce the children to the alien from Zog on pages 13 to 15. Encourage them to think of some questions they might like to ask the alien.
- Invite two children to write their question ideas on page 15. Highlight the capital letter at the beginning of the question word and the question mark at the end.

Independent work

- Give the children a piece of half-lined A4 paper. Ask them to draw a picture of an alien on the unlined half of the paper.
- Encourage them to consider what they would like to find out about their alien. Give some examples: *Where are you from? How old are you?*
- Tell the children to write their questions on the lined half of the paper.
- Remind the children regularly that their questions should begin with a capital letter at the start of a question word and end with a question mark.
- To simplify the task for less confident learners, provide the questions on cards, omitting the question marks, and ask the children to copy them and add question marks at the end.
- To extend the task, invite more confident learners to write a reply to each of their questions. Remind them that the answers will end in a full stop, not a question mark.

Plenary

- Invite a confident child to pretend to be the alien and allow the rest of the children to ask their questions.
- Scribe some of the questions on page 16 of the Notebook file, emphasising the question words and question marks. Ask the children to check their own work to ensure they have included question marks at the end of their questions.
- Scribe some of the alien's answers beneath the questions and ask the children whether a question mark is needed at the end of them.

Learning objective
PNS: Sentence structure and punctuation
- Use capital letters and full stops when punctuating simple sentences.

Resources
'Punctuation' Notebook file; half-lined A4 paper; pencils.

Links to other subjects
Science
PoS Sc1 (2a) Pupils should be taught to ask questions.
- Encourage the children to use question words and question marks when writing in science.
Speaking and listening
Objective 4: To explore characters through role play.
- Extend the role play by asking the children to take turns to be the alien, or to create other alien characters.

Whiteboard tools
Use a Highlighter pen to highlight the question marks. Use a Pen from the Pen tray to write words and questions on the board during the whole-class shared work.

 Pen tray

 Highlighter pen

 Select tool

Counting rhyme

Learning objective
PNS: Creating and shaping texts
● Create short simple texts on paper that combine words with images.

Resources
'Rhymes' Notebook file; writing materials.

Links to other subjects
Mathematics
PNS: Counting and understanding number
● Use the rhymes to help the children count from 1 to 10. Challenge them to think of rhymes for the numbers to 20. Ask them to rewrite their rhymes, using numerals instead of number words.

Starter
Open page 14 of the Notebook file and read the counting poem with the children. Ask: *What do you notice?* (The numbers counting up in order, the structure of the poem, the rhyming patterns.) Ask the children to highlight the rhyming words. Re-read the poem, asking them to listen for the numbers and the rhymes.

Whole-class shared work
● Go to page 15. Challenge the children to put the poem back together by dragging and dropping the words from the right-hand side of the page into the appropriate spaces. Point out that they could use the rhyming pattern to help them.
● Read the whole poem to check that no mistakes have been made. Point out that the rhyming words always rhyme with an even number word.
● Use pages 16 to 20 to explore other words that rhyme with the even number words (2, 4, 6, 8 and 10). On each of the pages, ask a child to name the number and the objects in the boxes. Together, decide which object rhymes with the number. Press the objects to check. If the answer is correct, you will hear a cheer.
● Think of other words that rhyme with that number and list them in the box.
● Referring back to pages 16 to 20 for word ideas, use the structure given on page 21 to model writing a new version of the counting rhyme.
● Encourage the children to contribute their ideas for each line.

Independent work
● Provide each child with a writing template for the poem similar to page 21 (or print out copies of this page).
● Ask the children to compose their own counting rhyme by adding the second line of each rhyming couplet. Refer them back to pages 16 to 20 for rhyming words they could use.
● Tell them to re-read their poems to check that they rhyme in the correct places.
● Simplify the task for less confident learners by providing them with a set of cards with one line of the counting rhyme written on each one and asking them to rebuild the poem in the correct order using the number words and rhyming couplets as clues.

Plenary
● Scan some examples of the children's poems into page 22 of the Notebook file. Invite children to read out their poems to the rest of the class.
● Ask the class to listen for the rhyming words in the poems, and share these at the end of the reading.
● Evaluate whether the poems followed the structure of the original poem and pick out lines that worked particularly well.

Whiteboard tools
Upload scanned images by selecting Insert, then Picture File, and browsing to where you have saved the images.

 Pen tray

 Select tool

Finding answers

Learning objectives
PNS: Understanding and interpreting texts
● Recognise the main elements that shape different texts.
PNS: Creating and shaping texts
● Convey information in simple non-narrative forms.
PNS: Sentence structure and punctuation
● Compose and write simple sentences independently to communicate meaning.

Resources
'Minibeasts' Notebook file; photocopiable page 55 'Finding answers', one for each child; pencils. (Microsoft PowerPoint is required to view the embedded slideshow in the Notebook file.)

Links to other subjects
Science
PoS Sc2: Life processes and living things
● Expand the topic of minibeasts by encouraging the children to find out how minibeasts feed and grow and where they live in the local environment.

Starter
Go to page 2 of the Notebook file. Ask: *What is a non-fiction book?* (A book that gives some sort of information to the reader.) Discuss what would normally be on the front cover of a non-fiction book and look at some examples. Ask: *What would you normally find at the front of a non-fiction book?* Encourage the children to explain the purpose of the contents page and how it can be used to find information. Write any key words on page 2.

Whole-class shared work
● Go to page 3 and open the electronic book.
● Show the front cover to the children and ask them to give the title of the book. Ask what type of book they think it is and what it might be about.
● Explain that to turn the pages of the book they must press the arrows at the bottom of the pages.
● Suggest looking on the next page to find out more about the content of the book.
● Confirm that the book is a non-fiction book about minibeasts and then read the book as a class. Discuss the text as you read it.
● Explain that the book doesn't need to be read in order and that by pressing on the hyperlinks on the contents page you can move straight to that page.
● Ask the children some simple questions about the book. Encourage them to go straight to the page that the answer is on, and highlight the relevant part of the text.
● When the children have finished exploring the electronic book, press 'Escape' on your keyboard to exit the slideshow.

Independent work
● Provide each child with a copy of photocopiable page 55. Ask the children to read the first paragraph quietly to themselves.
● Explain that the questions can be answered using information found in that paragraph.
● Support the children in writing an answer to each of the questions. Encourage them to write in full sentences if possible.
● Tell them to complete the rest of the sheet in the same way, by reading the next paragraph then answering the questions beneath it.
● Less confident learners should work with an adult, who can read the paragraphs and questions aloud to them while they follow with their fingers on their own sheets.
● Encourage more confident learners to write a paragraph of their own, and make up some questions for it.

Plenary
● Look at the reading comprehension as a class and share the answers from a range of children.
● Evaluate which answers were given in sentences and who gave the most accurate answers. Page 4 of the Notebook file can be used for assessment purposes.
● Encourage the children to make up their own questions that can be answered using the information on the photocopiable sheet. Invite the rest of the class to answer these invented questions.

Whiteboard tools
Use a Highlighter pen to highlight information in the electronic book.

 Pen tray

 Select tool

 Highlighter pen

Recount of planting a seed

Learning objectives
PNS: Understanding and interpreting texts
● Recognise the main elements that shape different texts.
PNS: Creating and shaping texts
● Convey information in simple non-narrative forms.
PNS: Sentence structure and punctuation
● Compose and write simple sentences independently to communicate meaning.

Resources
Big Book or prepared text recounting the planting of a seed; copies of digital photographs of different stages of planting a seed (one set for each group). Prepare a Notebook file: on page 1 show photographs of different stages of planting a seed arranged out of sequence; subsequent pages to show photographs in sequence, with space to write underneath.

Links to other subjects
Science
QCA Unit 1B 'Growing plants'
● Link this lesson with this objective.

Starter
Before the lesson begins, ensure that all of the children have had the opportunity to plant a seed. Ask them to recall the different stages that they went through when planting the seed and explain the process to a talking partner. Allow them to share their memories of the activity with the class, including any funny or unusual incidents that occurred.

Whole-class shared work
● Look at the Big Book with the children and explain that it recounts a seed being planted.
● Tell the children that it is a non-fiction text because it recounts something that has actually happened.
● Point out the features of the text as you read it. For example, it is written in the past tense and in time order, and uses time connectives.
● Open the first page of the prepared Notebook file (see Resources) and ask the children to look closely at the photographs. What do they notice? (The photographs are not in sequence.)
● Challenge the children to re-arrange the pictures so that they correctly recount the sequence of planting a seed.
● Show the children the second page and ask them to explain what is happening in the photograph.
● Model how to write a sentence below it, stressing that it is written in the past tense.
● Repeat this for the next pages, inviting the children to offer their ideas for sentences. Stress that you are recounting the events chronologically.

Independent work
● Give each group copies of the same digital photographs as those used in the prepared Notebook file.
● Ask the children to work as a group to arrange the photographs into the correct sequence.
● Invite each child to write a simple recount of planting a seed using the photographs as a memory jogger.
● Remind the children that their work should be written in the past tense and in time order.
● Provide a word bank of useful words that the children may need. For example, technical vocabulary such as *soil* and *trowel*, and simple time connectives such as *first, next* and *then*.
● Give less confident learners a prepared sheet with the photographs already in the correct sequence and a space to write underneath each one.

Plenary
● Invite the children to swap their recounts with a talking partner and read their partner's work. Suggest that they check that the recount they are reading is written in the past tense and in time order.
● Give the children time to list what was good about their partner's recount and suggest one improvement. Tell them to add a final sentence to their own work which states something personal about their experience – for example, 'I really hope my plant grows the tallest'.

Whiteboard tools
Use a Pen from the Pen tray or the On-screen Keyboard, accessed through the Pen tray or the SMART Board tools menu, to write sentences to accompany each photograph.

 Pen tray

 Select tool

 On-screen Keyboard

Rhyming words

■ Match the words that rhyme.

dog

van

fish

moon

man

hat

spoon

bin

bat

frog

chin

dish

CVC words

■ Add the missing letters.

s__n

ra__

__ot

cu__

ma__

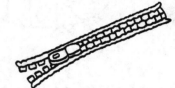

__ip

__ig

2 + 3 = 5

su__

ro__

ca__

wi__

__at

h__t

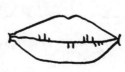

__ip

b__g

Illustrations © 2006, Jenny Tulip

Name _____

Colour mixing

- Mix some colours!

  ☐ Colour the clouds and write in the colour words.

  ☐ Use the word bank to help you.

blue	yellow	brown	purple	orange	red	green

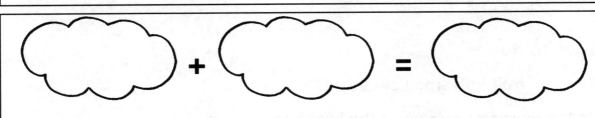

How to make a fruit kebab

■ **What you need**

- ☐
- ☐
- ☐
- ☐
- ☐
- ☐

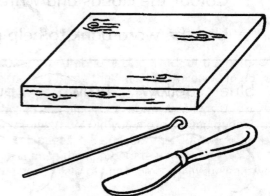

What to do

Chop the fruit into small pieces.

Put the pieces of fruit on to the kebab stick.

Eat the kebab and enjoy!

■ SCHOLASTIC
www.scholastic.co.uk

How to make a zigzag book

- Fold a piece of A3 paper in half lengthways and then unfold it.

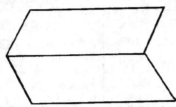

- Fold the same piece of A3 paper in half widthways and leave it folded.

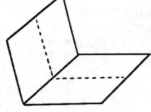

- Fold it in half again in the same direction, then unfold the last fold.

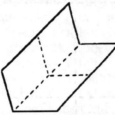

- Cut along the centre crease until you reach the middle of the paper.

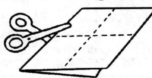

- Unfold the paper completely. There should be a slit through the middle of the paper. Fold the paper in half lengthways again and then push the two ends inwards towards each other to create a star shape with four arms.

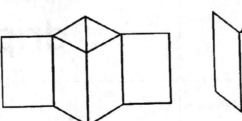

- The four arms are the pages of the book. Fold all of the arms around to face the same direction and the book is complete.

+r consonant clusters

☐ Sort these words into 'real words' and 'not real words'.

crat	brick
cron	grop
from	trust
prun	press
crab	drep
grin	trab
frass	drip
trim	breg

Pairing socks

◼ Put the socks in pairs to make words.

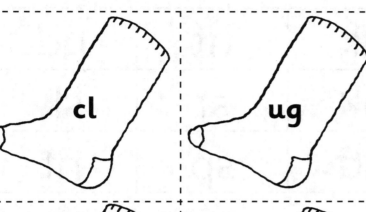
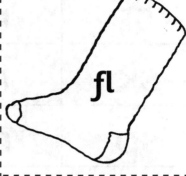

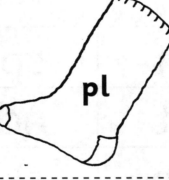
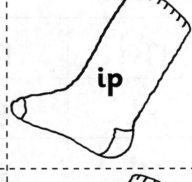

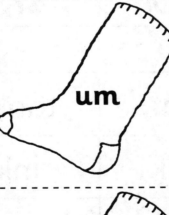
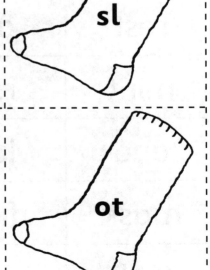

cl   ug   fl

ob   pl   ip

gl   um   sl

an   bl   ot

Illustrations © 2006, Jenny Tulip

Final consonant cluster bingo

Bingo board 1

st	nk	nt	nd
sk	nk	st	sk
sp	nd	sp	nt

Bingo board 2

nd	nt	sp	nk
st	st	nd	sk
nt	sp	sk	nk

Word cards

rest	ant	tank	gasp
mint	risk	sink	crisp
and	just	wind	went
mask	find	trunk	pink
tusk	wasp	task	mist

Design a superhero

◼ Make up your own superhero.

   ☐ Describe your superhero and draw a picture of him or her.

Superhero name:

_____

Real name:

_____

Clothes:

_____

Enemies:

_____

Super powers:

_____

Heroic actions:

_____

Describing old toys

■ Make a catalogue page for an old toy.

● _____

● _____

● _____

● _____

■ Write some sentences about the toy.

_____

_____

_____

_____

Long vowel graphemes: *ee* or *ea*

■ Add **ee** or **ea** to these words.

□ Make sure you choose the correct one!

sh_ _p

m_ _t

h_ _l

tr_ _

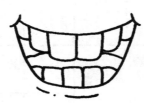

t_ _th

s_ _l

Don likes to f _ _ d the ducks on the pond.

The king had a big f _ _ st and invited all of his friends.

Sometimes I have bad dr _ _ ms at night.

The grass in my garden is gr _ _ n.

Kim's favourite food is vanilla ice cr _ _ m.

Jack climbed up a very tall b _ _ nstalk.

Name _____

Long vowel graphemes: *oa* or *ow*

■ Read the clues and fill in the answers to this crossword.

☐ All of the words have **oa** or **ow** in them.

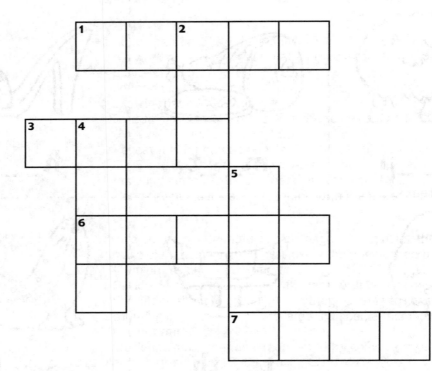

Clues

Across

1. Underneath.

3. A big black bird.

6. Shot with a bow.

7. Like a frog but bigger.

Down

2. Opposite of high.

4. Cars drive on this.

5. Wear this when it is cold.

Think of some more words that have **oa** or **ow** in them.

Long vowel graphemes: *oo, ew* or *ue*

- Read these sentences.

- Fill the gaps in the sentences with words from the word bank at the bottom of this page.

I sleep in my _____ .

We use _____ to stick things together.

My sunflower seed _____ very tall.

On a nice day the sky is _____ .

We wear football _____ when we play football on the field.

The bird _____ up to its nest.

At night, the _____ is in the sky.

A workman uses his _____ to do his job.

Word bank

blue	tools	moon	boots
grew	flew	bedroom	glue

Magic e

cat	tub	rod
win	stop	pin
man	hat	kit
past	van	dip
put	pit	cub
fin	cut	slab
cod	had	not
lost	clip	bun
rob	sum	plot
grim	tap	rip

SCHOLASTIC
www.scholastic.co.uk

Finding answers

Honeybees

A honeybee is an insect. It has six legs and one pair of wings. It has a yellow and black striped body. Honeybees collect nectar from flowers. They make honey from the nectar. People keep honeybees in beehives. They collect honey from the beehives.

Questions

How many legs does a honeybee have?

_____

What does a honeybee look like?

_____

What do honeybees make from nectar?

_____

Where do people keep bees?

_____

Butterflies

A butterfly is an insect. It has six legs and two pairs of wings. Butterflies drink nectar from flowers. They use their long tongues to reach inside the flowers. Butterflies lay eggs. The eggs hatch into caterpillars. The caterpillars eat lots of leaves. Then they turn into butterflies.

Questions

What do butterflies drink?

_____

What do caterpillars eat?

_____

Mathematics

The lessons in this chapter address objectives from the Primary National Strategy's *Primary Framework for mathematics*. Many of the lessons can be repeated at different times, such as lessons where the number range can be increased. In order to ensure that the pace of the lesson is kept sharp, lesson notes do not suggest that children write on the whiteboard themselves. If, however, some children are capable of writing clearly, then consider whether to encourage them to write up number sentences for the others to see.

Lesson title	PNS objectives	NLS objectives	Expected prior knowledge	Cross-curricular links
Lesson 1: Know these numbers	**Counting and understanding number** • Read and write numerals from 0 to 20, then beyond.	• Know the number names and recite them in order to at least 20, from and back to zero.	• How to count to at least 10. • The number names to at least 10.	**Geography** QCA Unit 1 'Around our school – the local area'
Lesson 2: Read this!	**Counting and understanding number** • Read and write numerals from 0 to 20, then beyond.	• Read and write numerals from 0 to at least 20.	• How to write numerals to 9.	**Science** QCA Unit 1A 'Ourselves'
Lesson 3: One more or less	**Counting and understanding number** • Say the number that is one more or less than any given number.	• Within the range 0 to 30, say the number that is 1 or 10 more or less than any given number.	• One more or less than numbers to 9.	**ICT** QCA Unit 1D 'Labelling and classifying'
Lesson 4: Larger number first 💿 🅿	**Knowing and using number facts** • Count on or back in ones.	• Put the larger number first and count on in ones, including beyond 10 (eg 7 + 5).	• How to order numbers to 10 and count on from any small number to at least 10.	**Geography** QCA Unit 2 'How can we make our local area safer?'
Lesson 5: Solving problems 🅿	**Using and applying mathematics** • Solve problems involving adding. • Describe ways of solving puzzles and problems, explaining choices and decisions orally or using pictures.	• Solve simple mathematical problems or puzzles; recognise and predict from simple patterns and relationships. Suggest extensions by asking 'What if... ?' or 'What could I try next?' • Explain methods and reasoning orally.	• Mental calculation strategies for numbers to 10.	**Science** QCA Unit 1C 'Sorting and using materials'
Lesson 6: Shopping 🅿	**Using and applying mathematics** • Solve problems involving counting, adding and subtracting, in the context of money, eg to 'pay' and 'give change'.	• Recognise coins of different values. • Find totals and change from up to 20p. • Work out how to pay an exact sum using smaller coins.	• How to recognise and name coins from 1p to 20p.	**Geography** QCA Unit 1 'Around our school – the local area'
Lesson 7: What can we find? 💿	**Handling data** • Answer a question by recording information in lists and tables; present outcomes using practical resources, pictures and block graphs.	• Solve a given problem by sorting, classifying and organising information in simple ways, such as: using objects or pictures; in a list or simple table. • Discuss and explain results	• How to sort sets by one criterion.	**Science** QCA Unit 1C 'Sorting and using materials'
Lesson 8: Comparing lengths 💿	**Measuring** • Estimate, measure and compare objects, choosing and using suitable uniform non-standard or standard units and measuring instruments (eg a metre stick).	• Compare two lengths by direct comparison; extend to more than two. • Measure using uniform non-standard units (eg straws, wooden cubes), or standard units (eg metre sticks).	• How to make direct comparisons of length, matching one end of each item to the other.	**Design and technology** QCA Unit 1B 'Playgrounds'
Lesson 9: Shapes 💿	**Understanding shape** • Visualise and name common 2D shapes and 3D solids and describe their features.	• Use everyday language to describe features of familiar 3D and 2D shapes, including the cube, cuboid, sphere, cylinder, cone..., circle, triangle, square, rectangle..., referring to properties such as the shapes of flat faces, or the number of faces or corners... or the number and types of sides.	• The names of 2D and 3D shapes and beginning to know some of their properties.	**Art and design** QCA Unit 2C 'Can buildings speak?'

Lesson title	PNS objectives	NLS objectives	Expected prior knowledge	Cross-curricular links
Lesson 10: Patterns	**Using and applying mathematics** • Describe simple patterns involving shapes. **Understanding shape** • Visualise and name common 2D shapes; use them to make patterns.	• Use one or more shapes to make, describe and continue repeating patterns.	• The names of common 2D and 3D shapes and beginning to describe their properties.	**Art and design** QCA Unit 1B 'Investigating materials'
Lesson 11: How many?	**Counting and understanding number** • Count reliably at least 20 objects, recognising that when re-arranged the number of objects stays the same.	• Count reliably at least 20 objects.	• How to count out objects to at least 6 with reasonable accuracy.	**Science** QCA Unit 1C 'Sorting and using materials'
Lesson 12: Tens and units	**Counting and understanding number** • Read and write numerals from 0 to 20, then beyond; use knowledge of place value.	• Begin to know what each digit in a two-digit number represents. Partition a 'teens' number and begin to partition larger two-digit numbers into a multiple of 10 and ones (TU).	• That teens numbers are made of a ten and ones and that these are represented by two written digits.	**English** PNS: Word recognition
Lesson 13: Number order	**Counting and understanding number** • Read and write numerals from 0 to 20, then beyond; use knowledge of place value to position these numbers on a number track.	• Order numbers to at least 20, and position them on a number track.	• How to order numbers to 10.	**Geography** PoS (1b) Observe and record (for example, identify buildings in the street and complete a chart).
Lesson 14: Partitioning	**Calculating** • Relate addition to counting on; use practical and informal written methods to support the addition of a one-digit number to a one-digit or two-digit number. • Use the vocabulary related to addition and symbols to describe and record addition number sentences.	• Begin to partition into '5 and a bit' when adding 6, 7, 8 or 9, then recombine (eg 6 + 8 = 5 + 1 + 5 + 3 = 10 + 4 = 14).	• What to add to 5 to make a total of 6, 7, 8 or 9.	**History** QCA Unit 2 'What were homes like a long time ago?'
Lesson 15: Number patterns	**Calculating** • Relate addition to counting on; use practical and informal written methods to support the addition of a one-digit number to a one-digit number. • Understand subtraction as 'take away' and find a 'difference' by counting up. • Use the vocabulary related to addition and subtraction and symbols to describe and record addition and subtraction number sentences.	• Use patterns of similar calculations (eg 10 – 0 = 10, 10 – 1 = 9, 10 – 2 = 8).	• How to use mental calculation strategies such as counting on/back in ones from the larger number.	**Art and design** QCA Unit 2B 'Mother Nature, designer'
Lesson 16: Number statements	**Using and applying mathematics** • Describe simple patterns and relationships involving numbers or shapes. • Describe ways of solving puzzles and problems, explaining choices and decisions orally or using pictures.	• Investigate a general statement about familiar numbers by finding examples that satisfy it. • Explain methods and reasoning orally.	• How to use mental calculation strategies for numbers to 10.	**Geography** QCA Unit 1 'Around our school – the local area'
Lesson 17: How shall I solve it?	**Using and applying mathematics** • Solve problems involving counting, adding, subtracting, doubling or halving in the context of measures. • Describe ways of solving problems, explaining choices and decisions orally.	• Use mental strategies to solve simple problems set in 'real life', money or measurement contexts, using counting, addition, subtraction, doubling and halving, explaining methods and reasoning orally.	• How to use mental calculation strategies for numbers to 10.	**Science** QCA Unit 1B 'Growing plants'
Lesson 18: Measuring	**Measuring** • Estimate, measure and compare objects, choosing and using suitable uniform non-standard or standard units and measuring instruments (eg a metre stick).	• Suggest suitable standard or uniform non-standard units and measuring equipment to estimate, then measure, a length, recording estimates and measurements as 'about…'	• How to make comparisons of length for two items.	**Science** QCA Unit 1B 'Growing plants'
Lesson 19: Seasons	**Measuring** • Use vocabulary related to time.	• Know the days of the week and the seasons of the year.	• The order of the days of the week.	**Science** QCA Unit 1B 'Growing plants'

Lesson title	PNS objectives	NLS objectives	Expected prior knowledge	Cross-curricular links
Lesson 20: Making models	**Understanding shape** • Visualise and name common 2D shapes and 3D solids and describe their features; use them to make models.	• Begin to relate solid shapes to pictures of them.	• The names and properties of common 2D and 3D shapes.	**Design and technology** QCA Unit 1D 'Homes'
Lesson 21: Odd and even	**Knowing and using number facts** • Count on or back in ones, twos, fives and tens.	• Count on and back in ones from any small number; in tens from and back to zero; in twos from zero, then one. • Begin to recognise odd or even numbers to about 20 as 'every other number'; count in fives from zero to 20 or more, then back again; begin to count in threes from zero.	• How to count in ones to at least 20.	**Science** QCA Unit 1C 'Sorting and using materials'
Lesson 22: Where does it fit?	**Counting and understanding number** • Compare and order numbers, using the related vocabulary.	• Understand and use the vocabulary of comparing and ordering numbers, including ordinal numbers to at least 20. • Compare two familiar numbers, say which is more or less, and give a number which lies between them.	• How to order numbers to 20.	**Geography** QCA Unit 2 'How can we make our local area safer?'
Lesson 23: Make a guess	**Counting and understanding number** • Estimate a number of objects that can be checked by counting.	• Understand and use the vocabulary of estimation. • Give a sensible estimate of a number or objects that can be checked by counting (eg up to about 30 objects).	• How to count objects to 20.	**Science** QCA Unit 1C 'Sorting and using materials'
Lesson 24: Does it matter?	**Calculating** • Recognise that addition can be done in any order.	• Begin to recognise that addition can be done in any order.	• How to use mental strategies for addition, such as counting on in ones from the larger number.	**ICT** QCA Unit 1F 'Understanding instructions and making things happen'
Lesson 25: Function machine	**Knowing and using number facts** • Recall the doubles of all numbers to at least 10.	• Identify near doubles, using doubles already known (eg 6 + 5).	• Doubles to at least 5 + 5.	**Design and technology** QCA Unit 1B 'Playgrounds'
Lesson 26: Making a ten	**Knowing and using number facts** • Derive and recall all pairs of numbers with a total of 10. **Calculating** • Use practical and informal written methods to support the addition of a one-digit number to a one-digit or two-digit number.	• Begin to bridge through 10, and later 20, when adding a single-digit number.	• How to use mental calculation strategies for totals to 10.	**Design and technology** QCA Unit 1C 'Eat more fruit and vegetables'
Lesson 27: Shapes statements	**Using and applying mathematics** • Describe simple patterns and relationships involving shapes. • Describe ways of solving puzzles and problems, explaining choices and decisions orally.	• Investigate a general statement about familiar shapes by finding examples that satisfy it. • Explain methods and reasoning orally.	• Properties of 2D shapes.	**ICT** QCA Unit 1E 'Representing information graphically: pictograms'
Lesson 28: Story time	**Measuring** • Use vocabulary related to time; order days of the week and months.	• Understand and use the vocabulary related to time. • Order familiar events in time.	• That events can be ordered, such as Sunday following Saturday.	**English** PNS: Speaking
Lesson 29: Telling the time	**Measuring** • Read the time to the hour and half hour.	• Read the time to the hour or half hour on analogue clocks.	• The o'clock times.	**ICT** QCA Unit 1C 'The information around us'
Lesson 30: Mazes	**Understanding shape** • Visualise and use everyday language to describe the position of objects and direction and distance when moving them, for example when placing or moving objects on a game board.	• Use everyday language to describe position, direction and movement.	• Which way to turn or move for directions of forward, back, left and right.	**ICT** QCA Unit 1F 'Understanding instructions and making things happen'

Know these numbers

Learning objective
PNS: Counting and understanding number
● Read and write numerals from 0 to 20, then beyond.

Resources
Counter software, available on the CD-ROM in the *Using ICT to support mathematics in primary school* training pack (DfES0260/2000); sets of numeral cards for ability groups (1-10, 1-15 or 1-20).

Links to other subjects
Geography
QCA Unit 1 'Around our school - the local area'
● Find examples of numbers in the locality (for example, house numbers). Ask whether the numbers are in number order, going up or down in ones, or sorted into odd and even numbers.

Starter
Open the Counter software (see Resources). Set Counter to count in ones, setting the start number to 0 and the step to 1. Set a steady speed, giving sufficient time for the children to read the display as well as say the number.
   Explain to the children that Counter will count in ones. Ask them to read aloud the numbers as they are revealed. Count to 10, then extend this to 20 over time. Repeat this several times, so that the children are confident with counting to 10, 15 and then 20.

Whole-class shared work
● Set the start number to 10 or 20, and the step to -1. Explain that you would like the children to count backwards, starting from 10. Start Counter and ask the children to count with it, keeping a good rhythm.
● Repeat the activity but this time stop Counter at some point. Ask: *What number will Counter show next?*
● Now repeat this, starting on different numbers (10, 15, 20) and counting back to zero.
● Ask questions, such as: *What is the next number in the count? And the number after that? What was the number before this one? And the one before that?*
● Finally, set Counter to count forwards/backwards again, and this time invite the children to take turns individually to say the numbers, keeping Counter's rhythm.

Independent work
● Ask the children to work in ability groups of four to six.
● Provide each group with a set of numeral cards from 1-10, 1-15 or 1-20, depending on the group's ability.
● The children take turns to choose a numeral card and count from zero to that number and back to zero again.
● When they have done this several times, ask them to start counting backwards from their chosen number to zero and back to the start number.
● Listen to their counting as they work. Check that they know when to stop the count, can say the number names in order, and count at a good pace.
● Limit the number range for less confident learners, counting up to 6, 10 or 12.
● Extend the counting range and numeral recognition for more confident learners, counting up to about 30.

Plenary
● Set Counter to begin counting from zero again. Increase the speed slightly, and invite the children to count along.
● Extend the stop point to one or two numbers beyond where the majority of the children have counted during the independent work.
● Repeat this for counting back.
● Now invite the more confident learners to demonstrate their counting skills, extending the range counting up to about 30.
● Repeat this, with Counter set at a slightly slower speed, inviting everyone to join in.

Whiteboard tools
Use the Counter software together with the Floating tools.

 Pen tray

 Select tool

 Floating tools

Read this!

Starter
Explain that you will say a number from zero to 9. Ask the children to write it in the air using their whole arm. Then write the numeral on the whiteboard, using a Pen from the Pen tray (set to draw thick lines), for the children to check. Clear the board by selecting Edit, then Clear Page, and repeat the activity, but this time invite a child to explain the movements needed to make the numeral.

Whole-class shared work
● Provide each child with an individual whiteboard and pen.
● Explain that you will say a number. Ask the children to write the number on their whiteboards. When you say *Show me,* they must hold up their boards.
● Invite children from each ability group to take turns to write the number on the class whiteboard.
● Begin with numerals to 9. Then extend to 12, 15 and 20.
● On a fresh Notebook page, add a picture of a strawberry from the Gallery and select Infinite Clone from its dropdown menu. Press on the strawberry and drag away from it to create multiple images. Ask the children to count the strawberries as you do so. Stop when you get to 10. invite a volunteer to explain what 'numbers' to write on the board to make 10, and then to write them. For example, to write 10, you need a 1 for the tens and a 0 for the units.
● Repeat this activity several times. Over time, extend the range to about 20 strawberries.

Independent work
● Discuss 'personal' numbers, such as age, house number, number of siblings or telephone numbers.
● Provide each child with a sheet of paper, a pencil and crayons. Ask them to write their personal numbers on the paper and illustrate them. For example, a simple drawing of a child with a 5 next to it can represent their age; a door with a 6 next to it can represent their house number, and so on.
● Tell the children that, for today, writing the numbers carefully and correctly is more important than the drawings, so that they do not spend too long drawing.
● Work with the less confident learners in a group. They can use the class whiteboard, so that they can make large numerals and 'feel' the shapes of the numbers.
● Encourage more confident learners to think of more numbers to write – for example, car number plates.
● Collect some examples of the children's work and scan it into the computer for the Plenary.

Plenary
● Show some examples of the children's work on the whiteboard.
● Invite the children to draw the numerals they see in the air.
● Invite individual children to write the numeral again on the whiteboard, using large movements.

Learning objective

PNS: Counting and understanding number
● Say the number that is one more or less than any given number.

Resources

Individual whiteboards and pens; sets of numeral cards of 1-20 for most children; sets up to 30 or beyond for more confident learners.

Links to other subjects
ICT
QCA Unit 1D 'Labelling and classifying'
● Invite the children to enter information into simple tables – for example, inputting quantities for a science experiment.

One more or less

Starter
Explain that you will write a number on the whiteboard. Ask the children to write the number that is one more than this on their individual whiteboards. When you say *Show me,* they should hold up their boards for you to see. Repeat this for one less than the number written. Keep the number range within 1 to 9. Extend the range over time to 1 to about 30.

Whole-class shared work
● Write this on the whiteboard:

Start number	one more than	Finish number
3	⟶	4

● Use a Highlighter pen to highlight the arrow and discuss that it means 'one more than'.
● Add numbers between 1 and 10 to the Start number column. Invite the children to say the Finish number each time, and note this in the appropriate column.
● Make another table, this time with 'one less than' in the middle column. Highlight the new instruction.
● Discuss this change, and ask the children to say one less than the number you put into the first column this time. Begin with single-digit numbers, and extend to 'teen' numbers.
● Over time, repeat this activity, extending the range of Start numbers to up to 30. The activity can also be used for 'ten more' and 'ten less' within the range 0 to 30.

Independent work
● Ask the children to work in pairs with a set of 1-20 numeral cards.
● They take turns to choose a card and ask their partner for 'one more than' that number. They record this using arrow diagrams, as in the whole-class shared work. Ask them to do this five times each.
● Now they repeat the activity for 'one less than' numbers.
● Limit the range of the numeral cards for less confident learners to 1 to 5, 8, 10 or 15, according to their confidence with the numerals. Extend the range to 30 or beyond for the more confident learners.

Plenary
● Write a new table like this on the board:

Start number	⟶	Finish number

● Point out that the arrow needs an instruction over it – either 'one more than' or 'one less than'.
● Put 15 in the Start number column, and 16 in the Finish number column. Ask: *Which instruction should go in the 'arrow' column? 'One more than' or 'one less than'?*
● Repeat this several times, so that the children understand that the words can be either 'one more than' or 'one less than'. Use pairs of numbers such as 17, 18 or 20, 19, and so on.
● Invite more confident learners to take turns to write the missing words on the whiteboard.

Whiteboard tools
Use a Pen from the Pen tray (set to a medium thickness) to write the numbers. Highlight the words that show the meaning of the arrow with a Highlighter pen.

 Pen tray

 Select tool

 Highlighter pen

Larger number first

Learning objective
PNS: Knowing and using number facts
● Count on or back in ones.

Resources
'Number tracks' Notebook file; photocopiable page 89 'Larger number first', one for each child; pencils; 1–6 dice and 1–4 numeral cards, for each pair of children.

Links to other subjects
Geography
QCA Unit 2 'How can we make our local area safer?'
● Practise the skills learned in this lesson by asking questions about the children's traffic survey. For example: *How many buses did you see? How many cars did you see? What was the total number of buses and cars?*

Starter
Display page 2 of the Notebook file. Point to each pair of numbers in order, asking: *Which is the larger number?* Ask volunteers to press on the number agreed upon. They will hear an 'aahh' sound if they are wrong, or a cheer if they are right.

Whole-class shared work
● Go to page 3. Invite the children to say the numbers from 1 to 10, in order, and ask for volunteers to write these into the track.
● Now write up the addition sentence 5 + 2. Point to the number 5 on the track and say: *To find 5 add 2, start at 5 and count on 2. So, 5, 6, 7. 5 add 2 is 7.* Point to the numbers on the track as you count on.
● Repeat this for other examples, keeping the total to about 7 or 8.
● Write 3 + 4 on the board and explain that it is easier to begin with the larger number. Ask: *Which is larger, 3 or 4?* Count on along the track, starting at 4 and counting on 3.
● Repeat this for other examples.
● Hide the number track using the Screen Shade and ask the children to try the next example mentally. Say: *2 add 5.* Agree that it will be easier to start at 5, the larger number. Say together: *5 and 6, 7. So 2 add 5 is 7.*
● Use the dice to generate other examples, with the children working mentally.

Independent work
● Give out copies of photocopiable page 89. Provide each pair of children with a 1–6 dice and a set of 1–4 numeral cards.
● Explain the activity: the children take turns to toss the dice and choose one of the cards at random. Then they make an addition sentence from the two numbers, putting the larger number first before finding the total.
● Decide whether to limit the number range for less confident learners by providing two sets of numeral cards 1–4.
● Extend the range for more confident learners by providing two 1–6 dice for each pair to use.
● Choose some of the completed tables to scan into the computer for the Plenary.

Plenary
● Ask the children to review scanned examples on the whiteboard.
● Invite individual children to say aloud how to total, starting from the larger number.
● Repeat, using other examples from the children's work.
● Try another couple of examples with the on-screen dice.
● Use page 4 to assess the children's understanding of what they have learned during the lesson.

Whiteboard tools
Use the Screen Shade to hide the number track when you ask the children to work out answers mentally.

  Pen tray

  Select tool

  Screen Shade

Solving problems

Learning objectives
PNS: Using and applying mathematics
● Solve problems involving adding.
● Describe ways of solving puzzles and problems, explaining choices and decisions orally or using pictures.

Resources P
Photocopiable page 90 'Solving problems', one for each child; eight counters for each of the less confident learners.

Links to other subjects
Science
QCA Unit 1C 'Sorting and using materials'
● Invite the children to sort different materials onto plates or into set rings. They can count each set, and, for small quantities, use mental methods to calculate the total.

Starter
Explain that you are going to write two numbers on the whiteboard, and you would like the children to add them together. Remind them to put the larger number first and count on in ones: 2 + 6; 5 + 3; 1 + 7; 4 + 5. Invite a volunteer to say the total each time, and to explain how they worked out the answer.

Whole-class shared work
● Explain that today's lesson is about solving problems.
● Ask: *How many different ways can we find for making the number 10?* Invite suggestions and write these on the whiteboard.
● Make a list of different ways of making 10. For example, 6 + 4; 5 + 5; 2 + 8. More confident learners may suggest some subtraction sentences, too.
● Ask the children to explain how they worked out their responses. Discuss mental methods, including putting the larger number first and counting on in ones. Change numbers round to put the larger number first.
● Repeat for another problem, such as: *I have some numeral cards for the numbers 1 to 6. How many ways can I make 7 using two cards each time?* Invite the children to suggest ways this can be done.

Independent work
● Give out copies of photocopiable page 90. Ask the children to work in pairs.
● Read the problem through, and ask for suggestions for solving it.
● Decide whether to provide counters for less confident learners to partition into the circles on the sheet. They can record their partitions as addition sentences.
● Challenge more confident learners, when they have completed the main task, to partition eight fish into three circles. They can draw and write their responses on the back of the sheet.

Plenary
● Invite children from each ability group to suggest solutions. Draw each solution and its number sentence on the whiteboard.
● Continue until all possible solutions have been found. These are: 0 + 8; 1 + 7; 2 + 6; 3 + 5; 4 + 4; 5 + 3; 6 + 2; 7 + 1; 8 + 0.
● Now invite the more confident learners to explain the challenge that they were set in the independent work.
● Ask all the children to think about how they could solve this.
● Draw and write solutions on the whiteboard. For example, 2 + 3 + 3; 5 + 2 + 1 and so on.

Whiteboard tools
Use the goldfish image in the Gallery for work in the Plenary activity.

 Pen tray

 Select tool

 Gallery

Shopping

Learning objective
PNS: Using and applying mathematics
● Solve problems involving counting, adding and subtracting, in the context of money, eg to 'pay' and 'give change'.

Resources ℗
Photocopiable page 91 'Shopping', one for each child; Toy shop software, available on the CD-ROM in the *Using ICT to support mathematics in primary school* training pack (DfES0260/2000); pots of 1p, 2p, 5p and 10p coins.

Links to other subjects
Geography
QCA Unit 1 'Around our school – the local area'
● Discuss shopping: where children shop with their families, and how they pay for goods purchased.

Starter
Place some pots of coins on each table in the classroom. Tell the children you are going to say a coin, and you want them to find one and hold it up. Say: *Show me a 1p coin.* Ask them how to write 1p, and demonstrate this on the whiteboard. When they are confident with recognising individual coins, ask them to show coins to make a total of between 3p and 9p. Record their suggestions as money addition sentences.

Whole-class shared work
● Display the Toy shop game, set to level 1 (see Resources). Explain that you would like the children to play this game with you.
● Say which toy is to be bought and point to the price on screen. Point to the coins and ask the children to say how much each is worth. Explain that the idea of the game is to make the price of the toy: they can use each coin as many times as they need.
● Ask the children to decide which coin should be chosen first. Ask: *What coin could I choose now?*
● Show the children that the total so far appears on screen. Ask them to suggest which coins they could use.
● Continue until the toy is bought for the correct price.
● You may wish to list the coins chosen at the side of the images on screen.
● Repeat this for another toy. The children may find it helpful to work with real coins as well, putting these in front of them and totalling for themselves.

Independent work
● Group the children in pairs. Provide each child with a copy of photocopiable page 91.
● Show an image of a toy on the screen. Each pair could take it in turns to choose a coin to add towards the cost of the toy. Give the children about five minutes to work out which coins to use, and to write a suitable money addition sentence.
● Review the different solutions to the problem. Write some different examples of money addition sentences on the whiteboard.
● Repeat the activity for another toy.
● Decide whether to work with the less confident learners as a group.
● Challenge more confident learners to find the way to buy the toy that uses the least number of coins each time.

Plenary
● Put the class into two groups and play the game with each group taking turns to choose the next coin.
● The group that chooses the last coin is the winner.
● Keep a running total of the coins that are chosen. Discuss which mental methods the children are using for totalling each time.
● Repeat this several times.

Whiteboard tools
Use a Pen from the Pen tray to record amounts of money.

 Pen tray

 Select tool

What can we find?

Learning objective
PNS: Handling data
● Answer a question by recording information in lists and tables; present outcomes using practical resources, pictures and block graphs.

Resources
'Bar chart' Notebook file; different items collected on a science nature walk (for example, leaves, stones and twigs); paper plates; small squares of sticky paper; large sheets of sugar paper; a collection of items that can be sorted in more than one way (for example, different coloured shapes that can be sorted by shape or by colour).

Links to other subjects
Science
QCA Unit 1C 'Sorting and using materials'
● Ask the children to sort and describe materials, then make a bar chart to show their findings.

Starter
Open page 2 of the Notebook file. Ask the children to name the days of the week and make a note of them. Discuss how it is helpful to make lists when collecting information. Ask: *What are the days of the week? How many have the same ending?* (All of them.) *How many begin with the same letter?* Make lists of the information on the board. Repeat for other types of information.

Whole-class shared work
● Provide each group with paper plates and items collected on the nature walk (see Resources). Ask each group to sort the items.
● Go to page 3 of the Notebook file. Ask: *How did you sort your items?* Check that the children have sorted them correctly (for example, into leaves, stones and so on).
● Use page 3 to make notes on how the sets of items can be combined – for example, all the plates of leaves, all the plates of stones. Give each group one set of items to count and ask them to write down the result.
● Go to page 4. Explain that the children are going to make a bar chart to show how many there are of each type of item.
● Invite each group to say what items they counted. Write this as a heading for each column – for example 'Leaves', 'Twigs'. Now drag and drop a block for each item counted. Discuss how the blocks fit together so that it is possible to see, without counting, which set has more items and which has fewer. Agree a title for the bar chart.
● Ask questions about the data, such as: *Are there more leaves or more twigs? Which set has most items? Which set has fewer than five items?*
● Use the Area Capture tool to take a snapshot of the completed bar chart.

Independent work
● Divide the children into mixed-ability groups of about four. Give each group a collection of items to sort, paper plates, a large sheet of sugar paper and small squares of sticky paper.
● Ask the children to sort their items onto the paper plates. They should then write headings for the columns of the bar chart, and stick a square of paper for each item in the correct column. They can then decide on and write a title for the chart.
● Challenge them to find a different way to sort the items, and repeat the activity.
● Ensure that each child is actively involved within their mixed-ability group and that the more confident learners do not dominate the work of the group.
● As the children work, invite them to explain how they decided to sort, and why.

Plenary
● Look at some of the children's charts.
● Ask questions such as: *Which set has most items? Which has fewest items? How can you tell? Which has more/fewer than ___?*
● Ask for volunteers to produce their charts using page 5 of the Notebook file.

Whiteboard tools
Use a Pen from the Pen tray to write up the lists. Use the Area Capture tool to take a snapshot of the completed bar chart.

 Pen tray

 Select tool

 Area Capture tool

Comparing lengths

Learning objective
PNS: Measuring
● Estimate, measure and compare objects, choosing and using suitable uniform non-standard or standard units and measuring instruments (eg a metre stick).

Resources
'Comparing lengths' Notebook file; construction kits; non-standard units for measuring, such as straws or cubes.

Links to other subjects
Design and technology
QCA Unit 1B 'Playgrounds'
● When making models, encourage the children to estimate then measure, using non-standard uniform units of length, and to make comparisons of height, length and width.

Starter
Open page 2 of the Notebook file. Ask: *Which worm is longer? How can we find out?* Agree that the two images can be placed so that one of the ends is level with the other, and a direct comparison can be made. Repeat for the other pairs of images on pages 3 and 4.

Whole-class shared work
● Enable the Screen Shade and go back to page 2. Reveal the first worm. Point out the squares on the right-hand side of the page, and ask: *How many squares long do you think the worm is?*
● Drag and drop squares along the image to match its length. Agree how many squares were used, and write: _(x)_ *squares long.*
● Discuss how the squares may not exactly match the length or height of an image, and that vocabulary such as *nearly* or *a bit over* can be used.
● Repeat the activity to find out the length and height of the images on pages 3 and 4. Discuss how closely the squares match for length.

Independent work
● Ask the children to work in mixed-ability groups of four.
● Provide each group with a construction kit and ask them to make some creatures.
● Provide some non-standard units for measuring. Ask the children to measure the length and height of their creatures.
● The children can record their measurements by placing a piece of paper by each creature with its length and height written on, and the units used.
● Ensure that each child is actively involved within their mixed-ability group and that the more confident learners do not dominate the work of the group.

Plenary
● Invite the children to order their models by length, shortest first. Remind them to keep the record of length and height by each model.
● Ask: *Which is the longest? How long is that? So which is the shortest? What did that measure?*
● Challenge the children to describe a model, in the form of *...is longer than... but shorter than...* Repeat this for height.
● Now ask the children to decide whether the order would be the same if the models were re-ordered by height.
● Ask: *How would you measure the width of each model?* Measure the widths and re-order the models, narrowest first.
● Ask the children to describe the position of their models in the row, in the form of *...is wider than... but narrower than...*
● Repeat this activity using page 5 of the Notebook file. Ask for volunteers to order the animals by length, measuring as required.

Whiteboard tools
Use a Pen from the Pen tray to record length and height measurements. Use the Screen Shade to show part of the screen at a time.

 Pen tray

 Screen Shade

 Select tool

Learning objective
PNS: Understanding shape
● Visualise and name common 2D shapes and 3D solids and describe their features.

Resources
'Shapes' Notebook file; 2D shape tiles; assorted 3D shapes; printing materials.

Links to other subjects
Art and design
QCA Unit 2C 'Can buildings speak?'
● Encourage the children to look carefully at buildings and to describe the 2D and 3D shapes that they can see.

Shapes

Starter
Open the Notebook file, enable the Spotlight tool and go to page 2. Show a triangle and ask: *What is this shape called?* Repeat this for the other 2D shapes. Then disable the Spotlight tool and use the Fill Colour tool to change the colour of each shape to black in turn to reveal its name, to check if the children's answers were correct.

Enable the Spotlight again, turn to page 3 and repeat the activity, this time using the Eraser from the Pen tray to reveal the answers.

Whole-class shared work
● Provide each group with a set of 2D and 3D shapes.
● Say: *I am thinking of a shape. It has straight sides. What shape could I be thinking of?* Encourage the children to sort the shapes.
● Go back to page 2 of the Notebook file. Ask for volunteers to sort the shapes with straight sides from the other shapes.
● Say: *My shape has three sides.* Agree that this is a triangle. Point out a triangle on page 2 and discuss its properties.
● Ask for volunteers to group all the triangles together.
● Go to page 4. Say: *Discuss this shape with the others in your group. Make a sentence to describe something about this shape.* Ask for responses. Write the children's sentences in the space provided.
● Repeat this for pages 5 to 7.
● Go back to page 3. Discuss 3D shapes, pointing out that these shapes have faces that are 2D shapes, such as squares and triangles. Highlight and label the 2D shape faces.

Independent work
● Provide each group with printing materials.
● Ask the children to choose a 3D shape and to print each of its faces.
● The children should write the names of the faces of their shapes.
● Leave page 3 of the Notebook file on the board, to provide vocabulary.
● The children should write a sentence for each of their 3D shapes, describing one of its properties.
● Decide whether to work with the less confident learners as a group. Encourage them to use and understand the vocabulary of shape.
● Challenge more confident learners to write more than one sentence to describe each shape.

Plenary
● Point to one of the 3D shapes on page 8 of the Notebook file. Ask: *What faces does this shape have?* Use a Highlighter pen to highlight the 2D shapes in the 3D shapes. Drag the appropriate 2D shape at the foot of the page and drop it under the 3D shape.
● Ask: *What sentence can you say to describe this shape?* Write a good example under the shape.
● Repeat this for the other shapes.

Whiteboard tools
Use the Spotlight tool to reveal the shapes and a Highlighter pen to highlight the 2D shapes in the 3D shapes in the Plenary.

 Pen tray

 Spotlight tool

 Fill Colour tool

 Highlighter pen

 Select tool

Learning objectives

PNS: Using and applying
mathematics
● Describe simple patterns
involving shapes.
PNS: Understanding shape
● Visualise and name
common 2D shapes; use them
to make patterns.

Resources

'Patterns' Notebook file; beads
and laces; coloured
interlocking cubes; pegs and
pegboards; coloured counters;
digital camera.

Links to other subjects
Art and design
QCA Unit 1B 'Investigating
materials'
● Do a weaving project, and
describe the pattern of
threads that appears. Invite
the children to spot and
describe patterns in their
clothes and other textiles.

Patterns

Starter
Go to page 2 of the Notebook file to reveal the first pattern of four shapes.
Ask: *What should I put next? Why do you think that?* Drag a square to
duplicate it and drop it into position, and ask: *What is next?* Pull down the
Screen Shade 🔲 and repeat this for the next pattern.

Whole-class shared work
● Go to page 3. Give the children coloured counters, and ask them to
continue the pattern until they have used eight counters.
● Say: *How would you describe this pattern? What comes next? And next?
What coloured circle should I put before the first one?* Together, add
circles to the pattern on the board until there are eight altogether.
● Reveal the second 'aabaab' pattern and repeat the activity.
● Go to page 4. Tell the children to look at the pattern carefully. Ask: *Is this
pattern correct? What is wrong with it?* Invite them to suggest how it
could be put right, and amend the pattern. (You can use the Fill Colour
tool 🔳 to change the shapes to the correct colour.)
● Repeat this for the second 'aabaab' pattern.

Independent work
● Ask the children to work in pairs.
● Provide each group with a set of pattern-making materials.
● Ask the children to begin a pattern. They then ask their partner to
describe the pattern and continue it. If there are sufficient resources, they
can keep their patterns to show during the Plenary. Alternatively, take
digital photographs and upload these to show during the Plenary.
● Begin patterns for less confident learners to copy and continue.
● Challenge more confident learners to make more complex patterns,
including those that build up as well as along.

Plenary
● Ask a child to show their pattern to the class, or show a photograph of one
that has been uploaded.
● Ask: *What is the pattern? How could you describe it? What would the next
... and the next ... and the next... [element] of the pattern be?*
● Repeat this for other children's work.
● Reveal the 'abcabc' pattern on page 5. Invite the children to explain the
pattern and say what comes next... and next... and to continue the pattern
on the screen.

Whiteboard tools
Use the Fill Colour tool to
change the colour of the
shapes in the whole-class
activity.

 Pen tray

 Select tool

 Fill Colour tool

 Screen Shade

Mathematics Lesson 11

How many?

Learning objective

PNS: Counting and understanding number
● Count reliably at least 20 objects, recognising that when re-arranged the number of objects stays the same.

Resources

'Build your own' file; photocopiable page 92 'Counting mat', one for each pair; items for counting, such as cubes and counters. Open the 'Build your own' file and prepare a Notebook file, showing sets of minibeasts (from the Mathematics folder under My Content in the Gallery) for the children to estimate and then count: the first page should show 5 minibeasts, the second page 6, and subsequent pages should show different quantities extending up to 10, 12, 15 and, over time, to 30.

Links to other subjects

Science
QCA Unit 1C 'Sorting and using materials'
● When collecting and sorting materials, invite the children to estimate how many before counting accurately.

Whiteboard tools

Use the 'Build your own' file, which consists of a blank Notebook page and a collection of Gallery resources located in the My Content folder, to prepare a Noteboook file (see Resources).

 Pen tray

 Select tool

 Highlighter pen

 Screen Shade

 Gallery

 Blank Page button

Starter

Go to the first page of your prepared Notebook file (see Resources) and ask the children to count the minibeasts. Invite them to explain how they did this. Check that everybody understands that each item is counted just once. Repeat for other quantities, extending to up to 10, 12, 15 and, over time, to 30.

Whole-class shared work

● Show the children a set of minibeasts and ask them to estimate or guess how many there are. Use the Screen Shade to reveal a set of six minibeasts for about five seconds.
● Ask for estimates, then reveal the set again and ask the children to count the minibeasts. Invite individual children to explain how they counted and in what order (for example, top to bottom, left to right and so on).
● Count together, highlighting as you go so that less confident learners can recognise what has and has not been counted. Then ask the children to find a different order to count the items.
● Repeat this for other quantities up to ten or more, depending upon levels of confidence in making accurate estimates. Each time, keep the 'reveal' time short initially, so the children cannot count exactly how many there are while they make their estimate. Invite suggestions for different ways of counting the items. Ask: *Does it matter in which order we count these? Why not?*
● Check that the children are becoming more accurate in their counting, and that they understand that it doesn't matter in which order items are counted: the count will always be the same.
● Over time, repeat this lesson, extending the range to up to 20, and then beyond that for the more confident learners.

Independent work

● Ask the children to work in pairs. Each pair will need a copy of photocopiable page 92 together with several counters or cubes.
● The children take turns to take a handful of counters and drop these onto the counting mat. They both estimate how many they think there are, then check by counting. Encourage them to count the items again in a different order, so that they understand that the order for counting does not affect the total.
● Use larger counting materials for less confident learners, as this will limit how many they can hold.
● Use smaller counting materials for more confident learners, as this will increase the quantity they can hold.
● Challenge all the children to find at least three different ways of counting each set.

Plenary

● Divide the class into two teams.
● Reveal a set of minibeasts on the Notebook file: the first team to say how many there are wins a point.
● Repeat about ten times, varying the number of minibeasts shown.

Tens and units

Learning objective
PNS: Counting and understanding number
● Read and write numerals from 0 to 20, then beyond; use knowledge of place value.

Resources ● ☐
'Tens and units' Notebook file; set of digit cards for each child, made from photocopiable page 93 'Digit cards'; writing materials.

Links to other subjects
English
PNS: Word recognition
● Provide stories for shared reading that contain numbers up to about 20, in both numeral and word form.

Starter
Provide the children with the first ten digit cards in the set made from the photocopiable sheet (0–9). Go to page 2 of the Notebook file. Read the story with the children. Ask them to look out for sentences with a number word. At the end of those sentences, they must hold up the correct digit card when you say *Show me*. Invite a child to come to the whiteboard and use the Eraser from the Pen tray to reveal the numeral at the end of the sentence to see if they were right.

Read the question at the end of the story. Count up the pictures of the presents together. Use the Eraser to check the answer. Invite the children to hold up the correct digit card for this number.

Whole-class shared work
● Introduce the cards for 10, 20 and 30. Discuss what the digits on each card represent – for example, 10 means 'one ten and no units'. Show the children how to make a 'teen' or 'twenty something' by placing one of the 0–9 cards over the zero place holder on the 10 or 20 cards.
● Go to page 3 of the Notebook file. Read each sentence, looking for number words. This time, ask the children to say as well as show you the numbers. Ask them to say how many tens and how many ones are needed to make the numbers. Invite a child to use the Eraser to reveal the answer.
● Count the friends to find out how many guests have been invited altogether.
● Repeat the activity on page 4.

Independent work
● Ask the children to work in groups of four. They will need the digit cards provided on photocopiable page 93, paper and pencils for recording.
● The children should write a sentence that includes a teen number.
● Display page 5 of the Notebook file, which provides the numbers to 20. Check that the children can spot the number word that they need.
● Decide whether to limit the number range for less confident learners to numbers up to 10.
● Challenge more confident learners to extend the range to 30. If necessary, provide a card with the number words written on it.
● Scan some of the sentences for the Plenary.

Plenary
● Begin by reviewing some of the children's sentences from the independent work. Invite everyone to read the number words and to show the numbers using the digit cards.
● Go to page 6 to finish the story of Mark's party. Ask the children to show each number word using their digit cards. Once they have done this, use the Eraser to reveal the answers on the screen.

Whiteboard tools
Use the Eraser from the Pen tray to reveal the correct numerals.

 Pen tray

 Select tool

Number order

Starter
Display page 5 of the Notebook file. Reveal the numbers slowly by pulling the tab on the left-hand side of the page. Ask the children to say each number as it appears. Point to one of the numerals and ask the children to draw it in the air. Watch to check that they do this correctly and invite a child who is confident at this to write up the numeral on the Notebook page.

Whole-class shared work
● Go to page 6. Point out the start number (1) in the first box. Say you would like the children to say what number should come next... and next... Write in the numbers to 10 in sequence, as the children say them.
● Use the Eraser from the Pen tray to remove the numbers from the track. Write the number 5 in its correct position on the track. Ask: *What comes one after/before 5?* Invite volunteers to come to the whiteboard to write in the missing numbers. Continue until all the numbers to 10 are in place.
● Erase the numbers in the track and go to page 7. Point out the 7 at the beginning of the track and the 12 in the final space. Invite the children to suggest what numbers are missing and where these fit. Write them in. Read together the numbers on the line and agree that these are in number order, even though this track doesn't begin with 1 or 0.
● Repeat the activity on page 8 for other number ranges, increasing the range to up to 20.

Independent work
● Give out copies of photocopiable page 94 for the children to complete.
● As they work, ask questions such as: *How do you know that this number fits there? What is the number one more/less than ___? Where would it fit on this number line?*
● Work with the less confident learners as a group. They can recite the counting numbers in order, from the start number until they reach the missing number.
● Challenge more confident learners to write numbers in order, from 15 to about 30, on the back of their sheet.

Plenary
● Show the ten-space number track on page 9 of the Notebook file, and write in:

	4			7			10		

● Ask: *How can we work out what numbers are missing?* Listen to the children's suggestions, writing in the one before and one after for each number. Then invite them to say what the last missing number is. (12)
● Repeat this for a different number range, such as 7 to 16.
● Erase the numbers in the track. Write 15 in the fifth space. Ask: *How could we find out what the first number will be? What about the last number?* Ask for volunteers to write in the numbers.

Learning objectives
PNS: Calculating
● Relate addition to counting on; use practical and informal written methods to support the addition of a one-digit number to a one-digit or two-digit number.
● Use the vocabulary related to addition and symbols to describe and record addition number sentences.

Resources
'Partitioning' Notebook file; photocopiable page 95 'Partitioning', one for each pair; number lines or tracks for less confident learners.

Links to other subjects
History
QCA Unit 2 'What were homes like a long time ago?'
● Invite the children to plan changing the home area into a historical room. They can make a simple plan and decide how many of specific objects they need. Remind them to total the number of objects using the mental strategies they have already learned.

Partitioning

Starter
Open page 2 of the Notebook file. Ask the children to suggest addition sentences that will give 6 as the total – for example, 4 + 2. Write the sentences on the board. Discuss how the children worked out their answers. Repeat the activity for 7, 8 and 9.

Whole-class shared work
● Go to page 3. Ask: *What should I add to 5 to make 6?* Write 5 + 1 underneath the strawberries, and demonstrate this partition using the strawberry images (you can add another strawberry by dragging one from one of the existing strawberries).
● Go to page 4 and repeat this process for seven strawberries: 5 + 2.
● Move to page 5. Write 6 + 7 = 5 + 1 + 5 + 2. Ask: *How can I work out the answer?* Move the white boxes together to encourage the children to combine the 5s in the top halves to make 10, and then add the 1 and 2 in the lower halves. Write 5 + 5 = 10, 1 + 2 = 3. 10 + 3 = 13. Demonstrate, and allow the children to try this using the strawberries.
● Write the total of 13. Say together: *6 add 7 is the same as 5 add 1 add 5 add 2, which is 10 add 3. The total is 13.*
● Repeat for pages 6 and 7 of the Notebook file. Add objects from the Gallery 🖼 or drag and drop the object at the top of each page.

Independent work
● Provide each pair of children with a copy of photocopiable page 95.
● In pairs, the children take turns to choose two numbers from the grid, write a number sentence and work out the answer. Remind them to partition each number into '5 and a bit'.
● Decide whether to limit less confident learners to adding 1, 2, 3, 4 to 6, 7, 8, 9. Work together as a group to practise counting on in ones: *6 + 4. 6 is 5 + 1. So 5 + 1 + 4 is 5 + 5.* If children do not know the answer, they should count on in ones to find it. Alternatively, they can use a number line to help them.
● Challenge more confident learners to total three numbers (such as 6 + 6 + 7) using the '5 and a bit' method.

Plenary
● Review some of the number sentences the children have written. Write these on page 8, without the answers. Challenge the other children to say how to work out the answers. Use counters from the Gallery if necessary.
● Divide the class into two teams. Explain that each team can choose two numbers from 5 to 9 for the other team to total. Give a point to each team for a correct answer.

Whiteboard tools
Use a Pen from the Pen tray to write number sentences. Select objects and counters from the Gallery for the Plenary, if necessary.

 Pen tray

 Select tool

 Gallery

Number patterns

Learning objectives
PNS: Calculating
● Relate addition to counting on; use practical and informal methods to support the addition of a one-digit number to a one-digit number.
● Understand subtraction as 'take away' and find a 'difference' by counting up; use practical and informal methods to support the subtraction of a one-digit number from a one-digit number.
● Use the vocabulary related to addition and subtraction and symbols to describe and record addition and subtraction number sentences.

Resources
'Build your own' file, containing 0-9 number buttons; pencils and paper.

Links to other subjects
Art and design
QCA Unit 2B 'Mother Nature, designer'
● When the children are studying design, ask them to search for patterns in what they see. Remind them that numbers can make patterns too.

Starter
Open the 'Build your own' file, which consists of a blank Notebook page and a ready-made Gallery collection of resources located in My Content 🖻. On the first page, put the number 4 as a number button (from the Mathematics folder under My Content) on the screen. Ask: *What two numbers could I add to make 4?* Use number buttons to illustrate the children's suggestions, ordering these 4 + 0; 3 + 1; 2 + 2; 1 + 3; 0 + 4 (or ask confident children to do this). Repeat this for other addition totals up to about 6.

Over time, repeat this activity for subtraction number sentences, such as 4 – 0, 4 – 1 and so on.

Whole-class shared work
● Put the button 8 on the board. Invite the children to suggest ways to make 8 and add the buttons to the board. Order the suggestions as number sentences: 8 + 0; 7 + 1... and so on.
● Discuss how 7 + 1 gives the same answer as 1 + 7. Invite the children to spot the other number sentences that have the same numbers in them.
● Now form the subtraction sentence: 8 – 0 =. Ask: *What is 8 subtract zero?* Drag in the answer. Repeat for 8 – 1; 8 – 2, up to 8 – 8.
● Discuss how these number sentences are in order from 8 – 0 to 8 – 8. Ask: *What number patterns can you see?*
● Discuss how the numbers are in counting order: 0, 1, 2 and 8, 7, 6...

Independent work
● Ask the children to work in pairs. Provide each child with paper and pencils.
● Invite them to write the pattern for 7 – 0, 7 – 1 and so on. When they have finished, ask them to work together to find the number patterns they can see.
● Ask them to do this again for 9 – 0, 9 – 1 and so on.
● Decide whether to work as a group for the less confident learners.
● Challenge more confident learners to write both addition patterns (7 = 0 + 7; 1 + 6) and subtraction patterns.
● Choose some of the work and scan it for the Plenary.

Plenary
● Display one of the pieces of scanned work from the independent activity.
● Invite the children to describe the number patterns they can see.
● Repeat this for another of the patterns.
● Ask the children to work with you to build the pattern for 10 = 0 + 10 on the board.
● Discuss how one column of numbers increases by one each time while the other decreases by one.

Whiteboard tools
Use a Pen from the Pen tray to write number sentences. Upload scanned images by selecting Insert, then Picture File, and browsing to where you have saved the images.

 Pen tray

 Select tool

 Gallery

Number statements

Learning objectives
PNS: Using and applying mathematics
● Describe simple patterns and relationships involving numbers or shapes; decide whether examples satisfy given conditions.
● Describe ways of solving puzzles and problems, explaining choices and decisions orally or using pictures.

Resources
Photocopiable page 96 'Number statements', one for each child; pots of mixed coins.

Links to other subjects
Geography
QCA Unit 1 'Around our school – the local area'
● Ask the children to collect information about prices in local shops – for example, what they could buy for 20p and different ways they could pay for this.

Starter
Write the number 6 on a blank Notebook page. Ask the children to think of addition facts that give the total 6. Write up their suggestions, ordering them so that the children can use what they see to find missing facts: 6 + 0, 5 + 1. Repeat this for subtraction facts, such as 6 - 0 = 6, 6 - 1 = 5.

Whole-class shared work
● Explain that in today's lesson you will be giving the children statements about numbers and you would like them to think of number sentences that show that the statements are true.
● Decide whether the children would benefit from having pots of coins in front of them for the first statement. Say: *I have two 2p coins and a 1p coin. I can pay for anything that costs between 1p and 5p.* Invite the children to think of money number sentences to show that this is true. Write what they suggest on the whiteboard, such as 4p = 2p + 2p.
● Say: *I can add amounts of money in any order. The answer is always the same.* Invite suggestions for this, such as 2p + 5p = 7p and 5p + 2p = 7p. Write up suggestions, with the two matching statements on the same line for the children to compare.

Independent work
● Provide each child with a copy of photocopiable page 96. Ask the children to work in pairs.
● You may wish to provide pots of mixed coins, to help the children decide on ways to answer the questions.
● Decide whether to ask less confident learners to draw the coins rather than writing money sentences to show their answers.
● Challenge more confident learners to show that it is possible to make 12p to 17p using three coins.

Plenary
● Invite a child to write their money sentence on the whiteboard for the first question on photocopiable page 96.
● Repeat this for question 2. Check that all amounts of money have been found.
● Invite more confident learners to explain their challenge, and how they solved it. The other children can count out their coins and check for themselves that the statement is true.

Whiteboard tools
Use a Pen from the Pen tray to write number sentences. Use a Highlighter pen to highlight key numbers and number patterns.

 Pen tray

 Select tool

 Highlighter pen

Mathematics Lesson 17

How shall I solve it?

Learning objectives
PNS: Using and applying mathematics
● Solve problems involving counting, adding, subtracting, doubling or halving in the context of measures.
● Describe ways of solving puzzles and problems, explaining choices and decisions orally.

Resources
'How shall I solve it?' Notebook file; photocopiable page 97 'How shall I solve it?', one for each child.

Links to other subjects
Science
QCA Unit 1B 'Growing plants'
● Make collections of things during a nature walk and use these to write number problems in the classroom.

Starter
Display page 2 of the Notebook file. Read out the question and ask the children to work out the answer. Write the number sentence 8 - 3 = 5 on the board. Ask a volunteer to explain how they found the answer. Ask: *Did anybody try a different way?* Discuss the different methods, if there are any, and their effectiveness.

Go to page 3 and read the question. Discuss different solutions and write down the number sentence 8 + 2 = 10.

Whole-class shared work
● Explain that in today's lesson, the children will be solving measuring problems.
● Go to page 4 and read out the problem.
● Ask: *How can we work out the answer?* Invite the children to say what the numbers are (4 and 2) and whether the number sentence to find the solution should be add or subtract. Invite a child to explain. Write 4 - 2 = 2 on the board.
● Go to page 5 and read out the problem. Again, ask what the numbers are, and whether this is an add or subtract problem.
● Ask: *How can you tell this is an add problem?* Agree that words like 'together' suggest add, and highlight this word. Write the number sentence 7 + 5 = ___ on the board, and ask for the answer and the mental strategy used to work this out.

Independent work
● Give out copies of photocopiable page 97.
● Read through the problems together. Ask the children to write a number sentence and then to find the answer for each one.
● Work with the less confident learners as a group. Encourage them to explain how to solve each problem.
● Ask more confident learners to write their own add or subtract problem for the Plenary.

Plenary
● Review the problems and discuss how children solved them. Write the appropriate number sentences on page 6 of the Notebook file.
● Invite more confident learners to read out their number problem. Challenge everybody to try to solve them.

Whiteboard tools
Use a Pen from the Pen tray to write number sentences and a Highlighter pen to identify key numbers in the sentences.

 Pen tray

 Select tool

 Highlighter pen

Measuring

Learning objective
PNS: Measuring
● Estimate, measure and compare objects, choosing and using suitable uniform non-standard or standard units and measuring instruments (eg a metre stick).

Resources
'Comparing lengths' Notebook file; sets of uniform non-standard units; items that can be measured (for example, small toys, pencils, brushes); paper and pencils; strips of paper; scissors.

Links to other subjects
Science
QCA Unit 1B 'Growing plants'
● Ask the children to choose suitable non-standard uniform units to estimate and measure the lengths and widths of items collected on nature walks.

Starter
Open page 2 of the Notebook file. Ask the children to say which of the two worms is longer, shorter, wider, narrower, and how they know this. Repeat for the other pairs of items on pages 3 and 4.

Whole-class shared work
● Enable the Screen Shade and go back to page 2. Reveal one of the images.
● Explain that you would like the children to decide which of the units on screen would be suitable for measuring the worm. Ask: *How long do you estimate the worm is?* Write down some of the estimates.
● Now drag and drop the chosen unit along the worm. Ask: *Was this a good choice of unit? Why do you think that? Did you make a good guess?*
● Repeat this for other items on pages 2, 3 and 4 of the Notebook file, each time asking the children to choose the appropriate units.
● Encourage them to use the vocabulary of approximation in their answers, such as *about, and a bit, nearly*.

Independent work
● Ask the children to work in mixed-ability groups of four. Provide each group with sets of non-standard units, so that they need to make a choice about the appropriate unit, and sets of things to measure.
● Ask the children to take turns to choose something to measure, and to decide which unit they will use to measure it. They should each make an estimate first, then measure and record their results.
● They can record their results in a simple table, for example:

I chose a...	My units are	My estimate is	My measure is

● Check that the more confident learners do not dominate the groups. Take time to discuss with the less confident learners the choices they make.
● Set the following challenge for more confident learners:
  ● Ask them to choose one of their units.
  ● Provide strips of paper.
  ● Ask them to cut a piece of paper that they estimate is about seven units in length. They can check by measuring.
  ● This can be repeated for other units and other lengths.

Plenary
● Go to page 6 of the Notebook file, which shows a selection of measuring units. Draw a thick line on the page.
● Ask: *Which units shall we use to measure this line? How long do you think it is?*
● Drag and drop units along the line. Agree a measurement, using vocabulary such as *about* or *5 and a bit*.

Whiteboard tools
Use a Pen from the Pen tray to draw thick lines on the Notebook page. Use the Screen Shade to reveal the images one at a time.

 Pen tray

 Screen Shade

 Select tool

Seasons

Learning objective
PNS: Measuring
● Use vocabulary related to time.

Resources
'Seasons' Notebook file; photocopiable page 98 'Seasons', one for each child.

Links to other subjects
Science
QCA Unit 1B 'Growing plants'
● Encourage the children to observe plants growing. Discuss the conditions needed for good growth. Ask the children to think about the seasons, which season is best for growth and why they think this.

Starter
Display page 2 of the Notebook file. Say together the days of the week. Write up today's name. Ask: *What day was it yesterday?* Write this above the name for today. *What day will it be tomorrow?* Write this under today. Continue to ask questions such as: *What day is next after ___? What day is before ___?* and complete the list of days of the week in this way.

Whole-class shared work
● Continue the work from the Starter. Ask: *Which days are at the weekend? What do you do at the weekend? On which days do we come to school?* Highlight the weekend days.
● Discuss how the days repeat each week. Ask: *How many days are there in each week?*
● Go to page 3. Ask: *What can you see in this picture?* Discuss aspects of the picture that give clues about the season (for example, the weather, the children's clothes) and use a Highlighter pen to highlight these.
● Write the name of the season clearly on the board: 'Spring'.
● Repeat the activity with the pictures on pages 4, 5 and 6.
● Explain that the seasons are like the days of the week and that they repeat in order. Reveal the current season page again.

Independent work
● Provide each child with a copy of photocopiable page 98. Ask the children to decide what season each picture shows, add more detail to each picture, and then label it with the season's name.
● Decide whether to work with the less confident learners and concentrate on ordering days of the week.
● Challenge more confident learners to write a sentence about their favourite time of the year.
● Scan in some of the completed work for the Plenary.

Plenary
● Use page 7 to display one of the scanned pieces of work from the independent activity. Discuss what the child has added to the picture. Highlight the features that reveal the season.
● Repeat for other pieces of work.
● Invite some of the more confident learners to read out their sentences.
● Invite everyone to say which is their favourite season, and why they like it.
● If there is time, say the seasons in order, from the current season. Repeat this for the days of the week from today.

Whiteboard tools
Use a Highlighter pen to highlight key days or seasons and features on the pictures. Upload scanned images by selecting Insert, then Picture File, and browsing to where you have saved the images.

 Pen tray

 Select tool

 Highlighter pen

Making models

Learning objective

PNS: Understanding shape
● Visualise and name common 2D shapes and 3D solids and describe their features; use them to make models.

Resources

'Models' Notebook file; a collection of 3D shapes for each group; paper, pencils and drawing materials; printouts of page 5 of the Notebook file, one for each child.

Links to other subjects

Design and technology
QCA Unit 1D 'Homes'
● The children can make models of buildings from pictures, and describe the shapes they used and how these fitted together.

Starter

Open page 2 of the Notebook file. Give each group an assortment of 3D shapes. They should sort the shapes, find the cube and name it. Ask: *How many faces does it have? What shape are they? How could you describe a cube to someone else?* Repeat this for other shapes in their collections.

Whole-class shared work

● Go to page 3. Invite the children to make the model with real cubes.
● Ask: *How many cubes are there? What shape have they made?* (A tower.)
● Take the on-screen tower apart and invite a volunteer to build it again.
● Use the shapes on page 4 to build a simple model. Then invite the children to build the model with their shapes. Ask: *How do these shapes fit together?*
● Repeat, making the model more complex.
● Give out paper and pencils. Make a simple model on the whiteboard and ask the children to make a sketch of what they see.
● Deconstruct the on-screen model. Ask the children to swap drawings with a partner, and then build the model using their partner's drawing. Invite them to discuss how easy this was and how the drawings could be improved.
● Invite a volunteer to rebuild the model on the Notebook page.

Independent work

● Display page 5 of the Notebook file. Provide each child with a printout of the page, paper and drawing materials, together with some 3D shapes for building.
● In small mixed-ability groups, each child should make their own model, and then compare it with the printout and with the models of the other members of the group.
● Next, ask the children to create their own model and to draw it on a piece of paper.
● Ask them to choose models from their group that they think are accurately made. These will be used in the Plenary.
● Ensure that each child is actively involved within their mixed-ability group and that the more confident learners do not dominate the work of the group.

Plenary

● Scan some children's drawings of models and display them.
● Compare two models that depict the same drawing. Ask: *How are these the same as the drawing? How are they different?* Encourage the use of shape vocabulary.
● Repeat this for other models.
● Invite the children to suggest some 3D shapes that could be dragged and dropped onto the screen to make a model. Obtain some 3D shapes from the Gallery and place them on page 6.
● Give the children a few minutes to make a model using real versions of these shapes. Compare their models with the one on the Notebook page.

Whiteboard tools

Use the Gallery to obtain 3D shapes in the Plenary.

 Pen tray

 Select tool

 Gallery

Odd and even

Starter
Ask the children to watch Counter counting (see Resources). Explain that you would like them to say how Counter is counting. Begin with counting in ones from any small number. When you stop Counter, ask the children to say what the next number will be, and the next, and so on. Repeat for counting back in ones. Then reset Counter, and repeat for counting from and back to zero in tens.

Whole-class shared work
● Explain that you would like the children to count with Counter. Set Counter to counting in twos, beginning on 0 and ending on 20. Repeat this several times.
● Now repeat again, this time counting back in twos from 20 to 0.
● Explain that the numbers the children have just said are the even numbers, or every other number starting from zero.
● Repeat, this time starting on 1. Explain that these are the odd numbers, or every other number starting from 1.
● Clear the screen. Ask the children to count, without Counter's prompting, even numbers, then odd numbers, forwards and back.
● Over time, extend this to include counting in threes and fives.

Independent work
● Ask the children to work in pairs. Give out copies of photocopiable page 99 and sets of 0–20 numeral cards.
● The children should shuffle the cards and take turns to pick one. They say whether it is odd or even. If their partner agrees, they keep the card and record the number on their sheet.
● When all the cards have been used, they order the numbers, 0 to 20, odd and even, on their sheet.
● Decide whether to limit less confident learners to numbers to 10, 12 or 15.
● Extend the range for more confident learners to up to about 30.

Plenary
● Set Counter to count in twos, from 1. Ask the children to identify the number pattern.
● Repeat this for counting even numbers, and then for counting in ones and tens.
● Over time, repeat for counting in threes and fives.

Where does it fit?

Learning objective
PNS: Counting and understanding number
● Compare and order numbers, using the related vocabulary.

Resources
'Number tracks' Notebook file; set of 0–20 numeral cards, one for each pair; paper and pencils.

Links to other subjects
Geography
QCA Unit 2 'How can we make our local area safer?'
● Visit the staff car park together, and ask the children to count the spaces for cars, how many cars are parked and to say how many spaces are left (or how many cars have been parked elsewhere because there is no room). Ask them to suggest ways to improve the parking situation.

Starter
Display the ten-space track on page 10 of the Notebook file. Write the number 1 at the beginning of the track and 10 at the end. Point to spaces and ask: *Which number fits here?* Ask the children to help you write the numbers into the track.
   Then use the Eraser from the Pen tray to erase the numbers and repeat the activity for other starting numbers below 6.

Whole-class shared work
● Reveal the 20-space number track on page 11 of the Notebook file. Write some numbers from 1 to 20 in their correct position on the track (for example, 2, 9 and 15).
● Point to the space before 2 and ask: *Which number goes here?* Repeat this for other before and after numbers. Extend to other positions on the track until all the numbers are in place.
● Leave the completed track on the whiteboard. Circle 6 and 9 and ask: *Which is more? Which is less? What numbers could fit between 6 and 9?* Agree that both 7 and 8 would fit.
● Repeat this for other pairs of numbers, between 5 and 20. Encourage the children to give a list of possible numbers.

Independent work
● Ask the children to work in pairs. Provide each pair with a set of 0–20 numeral cards.
● The children should spread the cards out, face up, on the table in front of them. They take turns to choose two numeral cards. They then both find a number which will fit between these two numbers.
● Ask the children to record their numbers: the lower of the two card numbers, then the number that fits in between, and then the higher of the two card numbers.
● Decide whether to limit the number range to up to 10, 12 or15 for less confident learners.
● Challenge more confident learners to search for all the numbers that will fit between their chosen pairs of numbers.

Plenary
● Using the ten-space track on page 12, explain that you will write two numbers on the board. Challenge the children to suggest all the numbers that will fit between these two.
● Begin with pairs of numbers with small differences, such as 7 and 11, or 9 and 13. Extend to pairs of numbers with larger differences, such as 3 and 12, or 5 and 14.
● Clear the numbers on the track. Write into the central space the number 14. Challenge the children to say the numbers that fit in the spaces that you point to, and write these in. Begin with either side of 10.

Whiteboard tools
Use a Pen from the Pen tray to write numbers on the number track. Use the Eraser from the Pen tray to clear the track each time, ready for the next set of numbers.

 Pen tray

 Select tool

Make a guess

Learning objective
PNS: Counting and understanding number
● Estimate a number of objects that can be checked by counting.

Resources
'Build your own' file; photocopiable page 92 'Counting mat', one for each pair; counting materials, such as cubes or counters. Before the lesson, open the 'Build your own' file and prepare a Notebook file showing different quantities of animals (selected from the Mathematics folder under My Content) to estimate and count on each page, starting with 10 cats on page 1 (choose quantities for estimating based upon the children's familiarity with counting out).

Links to other subjects
Science
QCA Unit 1C 'Sorting and using materials'
● Use a collection of materials, such as small pieces of different types of paper, card and fabrics, to make estimates, and count to check.

Whiteboard tools
Use the 'Build your own' file, which consists of a blank Notebook page and a collection of Gallery resources located in the My Content folder, to prepare a Noteboook file (see Resources). Use the Screen Shade to reveal images for short periods of time.

 Pen tray

 Gallery

 Select tool

 Highlighter pen

 Screen Shade

Starter
Open your prepared Notebook file (see Resources). Display the first page and ask: *How can we count these cats?* Invite the children to demonstrate how they would count. Repeat for other pages from the file, showing quantities between 10 and 20.

Whole-class shared work
● Enable the Screen Shade ▢. Explain that you will reveal one of the sets of pictures for no more than five seconds. Ask the children to estimate, or make a guess, of how many animals they think they can see.
● Ask: *How did you make your guess?* Discuss the strategies that the children used, such as looking for groups of two, or counting a few and guessing the rest.
● Now reveal the set again and ask the children to count to find how many animals there actually are. You may wish to use a Highlighter pen to highlight each item as it is counted, counting as a class. Keep a record of the estimates and count. Ask: *Did you make a good guess?*
● Repeat for the other sets of pictures.
● Now say: *I'm going to show you another set: do you think there are about 20 animals?* Show a page with about 20 animals for no more than five seconds.
● Ask how many the children think there are. Then check by revealing the image again and counting.

Independent work
● Provide each pair of children with a copy of photocopiable page 92 together with some objects to count.
● Ask the children to take turns to take a handful of objects, spread them on the 'counting mat' on the photocopiable sheet, and then make an estimate of how many they think there are. Their partner checks by counting.
● The children can record their estimate and actual count on a sheet of paper.
● Provide less confident learners with cubes, so that they reduce the quantity they take each time.
● Challenge more confident learners to take larger handfuls of smaller items, such as counters, in order to increase the number range.

Plenary
● Explain that you would like the children to play a game. Put them into two teams.
● Say: *I shall show you a set on the screen. One team makes a guess. The other team will count to check.*
● Keep the reveal time to no more than five seconds. You may even wish to reduce this time by now.
● Keep a record of correct responses. Note also who gives a reasonable estimate, and who counts accurately.
● Make a note of any children who need further experience of estimating and counting to check.

Does it matter?

Starter

Ask: *What number should I add to 7 to make 10?* Repeat the question, using other numbers, until all the totals for 10 have been covered. Then ask subtraction questions, such as: *What is 10 take away 4? What is 10 subtract 8? What is the difference between 10 and 5?*

Whole-class shared work

- Demonstrate Playtrain (see Resources). Explain that the two numbers at the bottom of the screen need to go into the carriages in order to make the total shown.
- Invite the children to suggest how to fill the carriages using the two numbers. Encourage them to total how many passengers have been put into the carriages after each number is pressed.
- Ask: *What if we put the numbers into the carriages in a different order? Will it make any difference to the total?*
- When the train is full, invite the children to work in pairs to suggest another way that the problem could be solved. This time, allow them free use of any numbers, but agree that the same number of carriages, and the same total, must be used.
- Discuss the solutions. Write these up as addition sums. Ask: *How did you work out the totals?* Discuss the mental strategies chosen and their suitability and effectiveness.
- Discuss whether the order of addition of the numbers in the carriages makes any difference to the total.
- Repeat this for other examples from Playtrain.

Independent work

- Show the children the next Playtrain game. In pairs, ask them to write down how many carriages there are, the two numbers they can use and the total.
- Invite the children to solve the puzzle.
- Now ask them to use any numbers they like from, say, 3 to 7, and to find other ways of filling the same quantity of carriages to the same totals. They can record as addition sentences, or draw the carriages and write the numbers in.
- Choose one of the ability groups to work with an adult using Playtrain set at a suitable level.
- Provide less confident learners with number tracks or lines to help them to total; alternatively, set them problems with the total at no more than 10 and using the digits 1 to 4.
- Challenge more confident learners to find at least ten different solutions to the puzzle.

Plenary

- Invite the children to demonstrate their solutions to the problem that you set. They can write their number sentences on the whiteboard.
- Invite the other children to check the totalling and explain how they added the numbers.
- If there is time, play the Playtrain game again.

Learning objective
PNS: Calculating
- Recognise that addition can be done in any order.

Resources
Playtrain software, available on the CD-ROM in the *Using ICT to support mathematics in primary school* training pack (DfES0260/2000) – set Playtrain to 'Easy'.

Links to other subjects
ICT
QCA Unit 1F 'Understanding instructions and making things happen'
- Show the children how to use a simple calculator. Ask them to input simple addition sums, predict totals, then press the '=' button to show if they were correct.

Whiteboard tools
The children can use a Pen from the Pen tray to write up their addition sentences and totals.

 Pen tray

 Select tool

Learning objective
PNS: Knowing and using number facts
● Recall the doubles of all numbers to at least 10.

Resources
'Function machine' Notebook file; 1–6 dice for each pair of children; paper and pencils; blank dice marked 4, 5, 6, 7, 8, 9 for more confident learners.

Links to other subjects
Design and technology
QCA Unit 1B 'Playgrounds'
● When using materials, encourage the children to calculate how much they need, using appropriate mental strategies to total. Include doubling, and doubling then adding or subtracting 1.

Function machine

Starter
Explain that you are going to toss the on-screen dice and that you want the children to double the number that they see. Keep the pace of this sharp, so that the children are encouraged to recall those double facts that they know. For those that they do not know, ask: *How could you work this out?* Write in the boxes on page 2 to show the original and doubled numbers if the children have difficulty with some numbers. Use the Eraser from the Pen tray to delete the written numbers and repeat the activity.

Whole-class shared work
● Go to page 3 of the Notebook file. Explain that a number goes in on the left side of the function machine. The function machine then doubles it and adds 1. The answer comes out on the right side.
● Ask the children: *What would happen if we put 3 in the function machine?* Drag the number 3 through the machine; it will change to 7 when it exits the machine. Did the children predict correctly?
● Roll the on-screen dice and write the number next to it. Ask: *What is double ___? And add 1?* Write the answer on the right side.
● Use the Undo button to erase the written numbers (or clear the page by selecting Edit, then Clear Page). Repeat the activity a few times.
● When the children are confident with this, repeat using the function *Double and subtract 1* on page 4. Again, drag the number 3 through the machine, asking the children to predict the answer. Use the on-screen dice to generate more numbers.

Independent work
● Ask the children to work in pairs. They will need a dice between them, and paper and pencils for recording.
● The children take turns to toss the dice and to say *Double and add 1* or *Double and subtract 1*.
● They both write a number sentence using the dice number (for example, 5 + 5 + 1 =, or 5 + 5 – 1 =) and write in their answers.
● Decide whether to work as a group with the less confident learners. You may wish to limit their work to *Double and add 1*, to begin with.
● For more confident learners, decide whether to provide dice with the numbers 4, 5, 6, 7, 8, 9.

Plenary
● Ask the children to look at the number sentences that you are going to write on the whiteboard.
● Go to page 5 of the Notebook file. Point out the number sentence 5 + 6 in the first space on the left side of the screen. Ask: *How can we work this out?* Discuss the fact that 5 + 6 is the same as 5 + 5 + 1, and 6 + 6 – 1. Ask the children to work out the answer, and to say which method they find easier and why.
● After writing the children's suggestions in the top white box on the right-hand side of the page, pull the tab across to reveal how the answer can be worked out by partitioning the numbers into '5 and a bit'.
● Repeat the activity using other similar examples (for example, 6 + 7, 4 + 3 and so on). Decide whether to extend the range to up to 9 + 10 in order to challenge more confident learners.

Whiteboard tools
Use a Pen from the Pen tray to write numbers into the function machine and the Clear Page function to clear them.

 Pen tray

 Select tool

 Undo button

Making a ten

Learning objectives
PNS: Knowing and using number facts
● Derive and recall all pairs of numbers with a total of 10.
PNS: Calculating
● Use practical and informal written methods to support the addition of a one-digit number to a one-digit or two-digit number.

Resources
'Number tracks' Notebook file file; photocopiable page 100 'Making a ten', one for each child.

Links to other subjects
Design and technology
QCA Unit 1C 'Eat more fruit and vegetables'
● Ask the children to keep a record of their consumption of fruit and vegetables during, say, three days. They then total the quantities by counting fruit, then vegetables, then combining these, crossing the 10 boundary as appropriate.

Starter
Say some addition sentences and and ask the children to say the answers. Use facts that they are beginning to know, such as complements to 10 (6 + 4, 2 + 8 and so on); addition doubles up to 5 + 5; all addition facts up to 5 + 5 (4 + 3, 2 + 4 and so on). Use the ten-space track on page 13 of the Notebook file if the children are uncertain. Discuss how the answer could be found by counting on in ones from the larger number.

Whole-class shared work
● Go to page 14. Write the numbers 1 to 20 into the track. Ask: *How shall we work out 6 + 7?* Agree that you could count on in ones from the larger number (7 + 6).
● Count on in ones from 7, and agree that the answer is 13.
● Explain that there is another way to do this. Write up 6 + 7 =. Then say: *We can make a 10 like this: 7 is the same as 4 add 3...* (write 6 + 4 + 3) *6 + 4 is 10, and 3 more is 13.*
● Repeat this for other examples that cross the 10 boundary – for example, 5 + 8 and 6 + 9. Each time, encourage the children to use the new method first, and write up the expanded number sentence. Check by counting along the number track, beginning with the larger number.

Independent work
● Give out copies of photocopiable page 100. In pairs, the children should make eight number sentences using the numbers on the sheet, and work them out using the new method.
● Decide whether to work with the less confident learners as a group. Encourage them to use mental strategies, then to check their answers counting on in ones from the larger number, either mentally or using a number track.
● Challenge more confident learners to try some examples that cross the 20 boundary, such as 19 + 3 or 17 + 6.

Plenary
● Go to page 15. Invite a volunteer to read out a number sentence, without giving the expanded number sentence or the answer. Write it up and ask the other children to decide how to work out the problem. Write out the relevant expanded number sentence. For example, 6 + 8 = 6 + 4 + 4 = 10 + 4 = 14.
● Repeat for other examples.
● Over time, extend this to crossing the 20 boundary.

Whiteboard tools
Use a Pen from the Pen tray to write numbers into the number track and the Eraser to erase them.

 Pen tray

 Select tool

Learning objectives
PNS: Using and applying mathematics
● Describe simple patterns and relationships involving shapes; decide whether examples satisfy given conditions.
● Describe ways of solving puzzles and problems, explaining choices and decisions orally.

Resources
'Shapes' Notebook file; individual whiteboards and pens; sets of assorted 2D shapes (including different examples of squares, rectangles and triangles), one set for each group of four to six; large piece of paper and pencils for recording.

Links to other subjects
ICT
QCA Unit 1E 'Representing information graphically: pictograms'
● The children can sort sets of shapes into 'same shape' sets, then record their findings in a pictogram.

Shapes statements

Starter
Open page 2 of the Notebook file. Enable the Spotlight tool and focus on one of the shapes. Ask the children to name the shape and ask questions about its properties. For example, for a triangle children can say it has three straight sides and three angles. Repeat for other 2D shapes on page 2, and for 3D shapes on page 3.

Whole-class shared work
● Provide each child with an individual whiteboard and pen.
● Spotlight a triangle on page 2. Say: *All triangles have three sides. Is this true?* Ask the children to draw a triangle, and to hold up their whiteboards when you say *Show me*. Check that everyone has drawn a triangle.
● Now invite the children to look at others' drawings. Ask: *Do all triangles have three sides?*
● Go to page 9, so that the children can see a right-angled, scalene, equilateral and isosceles triangle.
● Agree that all the triangles have the same number of sides.
● Ask: *What else do triangles have?* Agree that they all have straight sides and three angles. Write this on the board.
● Repeat this activity for the circles on page 10.

Independent work
● Explain that you would like the children to find examples for these statements:
  ● All rectangles have four straight sides.
  ● All circles have a curved side.
  ● All triangles have three angles.
● In groups of four to six, the children should sort the 2D shapes in the box on their table. They can record by choosing the appropriate shapes and drawing around them on paper.
● Decide whether to work with the less confident learners as a group. Encourage them to use the vocabulary of shape to describe the shapes they sort, focusing on how these are the same or different.
● Challenge more confident learners to find an example for this statement: *All the squares of the same size fit together, leaving no gaps.*

Plenary
● Invite children from each ability group to show examples of their work to the rest of the class. Ask them to explain how their shapes fit the statement.
● Go to page 11. Ask: *What are these? What sentence can you say that tells me about these shapes?* Agree that all rectangles have four straight sides.
● Discuss how rectangles have opposite sides the same length.
● Go back to page 2, and ask for volunteers to sort the shapes into triangles rectangles, circle and square.
● Over time, repeat this work for 3D shapes.

Whiteboard tools
Use a Pen from the Pen tray to write down the properties of shapes. Use the Spotlight tool to highlight individual shapes in the Starter.

 Pen tray

 Spotlight tool

 Select tool

Story time

Learning objective
PNS: Measuring
● Use vocabulary related to time; order days of the week and months.

Resources
'Story time' Notebook file; photocopiable page 101 'Story time', one for each child; scissors; glue; paper; individual whiteboards and pens.

Links to other subjects
English
PNS: Speaking
● Encourage the children to retell stories, ordering the events in sequence.

Starter
Ask: *What day is it today?* Write this on page 2 of the Notebook file. Now say: *What day was it yesterday? What day will it be tomorrow? Which days do we come to school? Which days do we stay at home?* Now ask about the seasons: *What season is it now? How can we tell? What comes after this season? How can we tell that season?*

Whole-class shared work
● Explain that you will show the children some pictures with words underneath.
● Go to page 3 of the Notebook file. Point to the first picture and ask: *What can you tell me about this picture?* Discuss what the children can see, what time of day it is, and what the child is doing. Read the sentences together. Decide where the first picture belongs and move it there (to help the children reach the correct decision, allow them to vote by writing on individual whiteboards).
● Repeat this for the other pictures. Ask: *Are these pictures in order? Does Jamie eat his lunch first at school? Why not?* Use a Highlighter pen to highlight the clocks in each picture.
● Order the pictures as the children direct you, dragging and dropping them into place.
● When the pictures have been ordered, look again with the children at each picture. Ask: *What do the clocks show? Are these in order now?* Read the sentences together to check that the pictures are in order.
● Repeat this for the pictures and sentences on page 4.

Independent work
● Provide each child with a copy of photocopiable page 101 and a blank sheet of paper. Each group also needs scissors and glue.
● Ask the children to cut out the pictures on the photocopiable sheet, then to decide on their order to tell the story. They should glue the pictures, in order, onto a fresh sheet of paper.
● Provide a second sheet of paper for each child. Ask the children to think of a story and to draw four pictures to illustrate it. They should then cut the pictures apart and swap with another child. Each child should reassemble the pictures in story order, then discuss with the other child whether or not they have ordered the pictures correctly.
● Decide whether to use an A3 enlargement of the photocopiable sheet, and work with the less confident learners as a group to order the pictures.
● Challenge more confident learners to produce more complicated illustrated stories, with six pictures.
● Scan examples of the children's work from the second task into the computer, for use during the Plenary.

Plenary
● Go to page 5 of the Notebook file. Ask a child to order the pictures on screen by dragging and dropping them into the correct position.
● Use page 6 to display a completed, ordered set of pictures from the second part of the independent work. Discuss what the pictures show and how the children knew how to order them.
● Repeat this for other examples.

Whiteboard tools
Use a Highlighter pen to highlight the clock faces, or other key facts, in the pictures. Upload scanned images by selecting Insert, then Picture File, and browsing to where you have saved the images.

 Pen tray

 Highlighter pen

 Select tool

Telling the time

Learning objective
PNS: Measuring
● Read the time to the hour and half hour.

Resources
'Telling the time' Notebook file; a set of cards for each pair made up from photocopiable page 102 'Telling the time' (you may wish to write the correct time on the back of each card, if children are not confident with telling the time); teaching clock face; individual clock faces, one for each child.

Links to other subjects
ICT
QCA Unit 1C 'The information around us'
● Ask the children to collect pictures of different clock faces. Discuss the range of clock faces available and, where the times are o'clock or half past, ask the children to say the times.

Starter
Open page 2 of the Notebook file. Look at the clock faces, and agree that all of them show o'clock times. Ask the children to set their individual clock faces to the first time and to show you. Together, say what time that is. Repeat this for the other times shown on pages 3 to 6. Invite a child to remove each box to reveal the correct time.

Whole-class shared work
● Use the teaching clock to show the children how the clock hands are set for 2.30. Say: *This clock shows half past two. The minute hand is pointing to the six, so that we know it is a half-past time.* Elicit from the children that the hour hand is pointing to mid-way between the 2 and the 3.
● Go to page 7 of the Notebook file. Again, ask the children to set their individual clock faces to match this set of clocks. For each time, check that the children set their clocks accurately, and can say the time. Remove the boxes to reveal the correct time.
● Invite a child to describe the position of the hands for each half-past time.
● Repeat the activity on pages 8 to 11.

Independent work
● Give each pair of children a set of cards made from photocopiable page 102, and ask them to shuffle the pack. Give less confident learners cards with the correct times written on the back.
● They take turns to take a card and ask their partner to say the time on the card.
● They repeat this until all the cards have been used.
● Challenge the children to order the clock times starting with 1 o'clock.
● Provide less confident learners with individual clock faces. Ask the children to set their clock face to each time shown on the cards, as well as reading the times.
● Challenge more confident learners to choose some times that are important to them, and to be ready to say during the Plenary what they do at these times. This could include the time they get up, leave home in the morning or go to bed at night.

Plenary
● Go to page 12. Repeat the activity from the Starter. Note that these are a mixture of o'clock and half-past times.
● Repeat the activity on pages 13 to 16.
● Invite more confident learners to say one of their times, and talk about why it is important to them. Ask the other children to set their clocks to this time.

Whiteboard tools

 Pen tray

 Select tool

Mazes

Starter
Carry out the Starter in a space where the children can move freely. Say: *I am going to give you some instructions for moving and turning. Listen carefully, then follow the instructions.*
Begin with simple, one-move instructions, such as: *Turn right; turn left; take one pace forward/back...* When the children are confident with this, give more complex instructions that involve two actions, such as: *Move forward three steps then turn right...* If the children are unsure of which is their left or right side, consider giving them something to hold in their right hand so that they can identify this side of themselves with ease.

Whole-class shared work
● Go to page 2 of the Notebook file. Ask the children to look carefully at the maze. Explain that you would like them to decide how to move the child (in the bottom left-hand corner) from home to the school. Invite them to give directions for doing this.
● The children will not be able to give a specific distance instruction, but should be able to say, for example: *Move forward; turn right/left at the bend...* Use a Highlighter pen to highlight the route according to their instructions. Then move the child to the final place following the route (or invite a child to do so).
● Invite the children to give other suggestions for moving the child from home to school.
● Repeat this for other moves between two points on the Notebook page.

Independent work
● Provide each pair of children with a copy of photocopiable page 103. Tell them to take turns to decide which animal is to go home. Their partner finds and describes a route for the animal to get home.
● When they have sent all the animals home, they should decide on another animal, draw the animal and its home on the sheet, and then find a way for their animal to get home.
● Decide whether to work with the less confident learners as a group. Help them to develop the vocabulary of position and movement.
● Challenge more confident learners to give instructions for visiting each home in turn.

Plenary
● Go to page 3 and ask the children to give instructions for moving between two of the attractions at the zoo.
● Invite the children to choose two types of animals to visit. They should describe the route to their neighbour, preparing to describe this to the class.
● Choose some children to describe their routes. Follow their routes with a Highlighter pen and ask the other children if they agree with the chosen route.
● Finally, tell the children that the zoo will be closing soon. Ask them to describe the route to the car park.

Name _____

Larger number first

- ◾ You will need:
  - ▢ A dice
  - ▢ A set of 1–4 numeral cards
- ◾ Work with a partner.
  - ▢ Take turns to throw the dice and choose a number card.
  - ▢ Use the two numbers to write an addition sentence. Remember to put the larger number first.
- ◾ Write the total.

Dice	Card	Addition sentence (larger number first)	Total

Solving problems

■ Here are eight fish.

  ☐ Find different ways to put eight fish into two circles.

■ Record each way you find by drawing the fish into the circles below.

  ☐ Write an addition sentence to show what you have done.

◯ ◯ ◯ ◯

☐ + ☐ = ☐   ☐ + ☐ = ☐

◯ ◯ ◯ ◯

☐ + ☐ = ☐   ☐ + ☐ = ☐

◯ ◯ ◯ ◯

☐ + ☐ = ☐   ☐ + ☐ = ☐

■ SCHOLASTIC
w w w . s c h o l a s t i c . c o . u k

Illustrations © 2006, Jenny Tulip

Name _____

Shopping

- You will need a pot of 1p, 2p, 5p and 10p coins.

  - Work with a partner.

  - Look at the toy on screen and write its name.

  - Decide with your partner which coins to use to pay for the toy.

- Write a money addition sentence.

Toy	Coins	Money addition sentence

Counting mat

Digit cards

1 0   2 0   3 0

1   2   3

4   5   6

7   8   9

Name _____

Number track

1. Write in the missing numbers.

1 , 2 , ▢ , ▢ , ▢ , 6

3 , ▢ , ▢ , ▢ , 7 , 8

6 , 7 , ▢ , ▢ , 10 , ▢

▢ , ▢ , 7 , 8 , ▢ , 10

2. Write where these numbers will fit on the track.

5   9   2   4

1									10

11   6   8   7

3									12

12   10   7   14

6									15

3. Write the numbers from 1 to 20 in this track.

1									10

4. Write in the missing numbers on these tracks.

		6						12	

	7							13	

100 SMART Board™ LESSONS • YEAR 1

◣ S C H O L A S T I C
w w w . s c h o l a s t i c . c o . u k

Partitioning

■ Work with a partner.

   □ Take turns to choose two numbers on the grid.

   □ Write a number sentence and work out the answer.

   □ The other player checks the answer.

   □ Cross out the numbers you chose.

6	6	6
7	7	7
8	8	8
9	9	9

Player 1

5 + [   ] + 5 + [   ] = 10 + [   ] = [   ]

5 + [   ] + 5 + [   ] = 10 + [   ] = [   ]

5 + [   ] + 5 + [   ] = 10 + [   ] = [   ]

Player 2

5 + [   ] + 5 + [   ] = 10 + [   ] = [   ]

5 + [   ] + 5 + [   ] = 10 + [   ] = [   ]

5 + [   ] + 5 + [   ] = 10 + [   ] = [   ]

Number statements

- Work with a partner.

  □ Write some money number sentences for each of these statements.

1. Sandeep wants to buy an orange for 6p.

He can pay 6p with no change.

Write different ways he can do this.

2. Fay has the coins 1p, 2p, 2p and 5p.

She can make any amount from 1p to 10p.

Write the ways she can do this.

Illustrations © 2006, Jenny Tulip

SCHOLASTIC
www.scholastic.co.uk

How shall I solve it?

■ Read the problem.

  ☐ Write a number sentence.

  ☐ Write the answer.

1. Paul collects some conkers.

   There are six conkers in one box.

   There are eight conkers in the other box.

   How many conkers are there altogether?

2. Jody collects two sticks.

   One stick is four bricks long.

   The other stick is nine bricks long.

   How long are the two sticks in total?

3. Sarah balances all her leaves with 12 bricks.

   She put some of her leaves on to the balance.

   These leaves balance with seven bricks.

   How many bricks will balance the rest of Sarah's leaves?

Seasons

- ◢ Decide which of these pictures shows spring.
  - ☐ Finish the picture.
- ◢ Now do the same for summer, autumn and winter.
  - ☐ Write the name of the season for each picture.

Illustrations © 2006, Jenny Tulip

Odd or even?

- ● Work with a partner.
    - ☐ Take turns to pick a numeral card.
    - ☐ Decide whether your number is odd or even.
    - ☐ Write it into the right box.

Odd	Even

- ● Now sort the odd numbers.
    - ☐ Write them again in order.
    - ☐ Do this again for the even numbers.

These odd numbers are in number order	These even numbers are in number order

Making a ten

■ Work with a partner.

☐ Take turns to choose two numbers from the box.

☐ Write a number sentence.

☐ Both of you work out the answer.

☐ Repeat this, until you have eight different number sentences.

6	7	8	9

_____ + _____ = _____

_____ + _____ = _____

_____ + _____ = _____

_____ + _____ = _____

_____ + _____ = _____

_____ + _____ = _____

_____ + _____ = _____

_____ + _____ = _____

Story time

■ You will need scissors, glue and paper.

☐ Cut out each picture.

☐ Look at the pictures.

☐ Read the words under the pictures.

☐ Put the pictures in order.

☐ Glue the pictures in order onto a piece of paper.

Clare throws the ball
for her puppy.

The puppy chases the ball.

Clare helps the puppy
to get the ball.

The puppy cannot get the ball.

Telling the time

100 SMART Board™ LESSONS • YEAR 1

▟ **SCHOLASTIC**
www.scholastic.co.uk

Animal homes

- Work with a partner.

  ☐ Take turns to choose an animal and its home.

  ☐ Now ask your partner to tell you how the animal could get home.

- Think of another animal.

  ☐ Draw it on the maze.

  ☐ Now draw its home.

  ☐ Find a way for the animal to get home.

Illustrations © 2006, Jenny Tulip

Science

This chapter provides 20 lessons based on objectives taken from the QCA Schemes of Work for science. The lessons cover a range of objectives from each of the six units of work for Year 1. The lessons show how the interactive whiteboard can be used to teach and model new scientific concepts to the whole class. There are lots of opportunities for children to develop their investigative skills by allowing them to share and discuss ideas. The lessons also provide children with opportunities to be actively involved in using the whiteboard by selecting, moving and sorting images and text, writing or typing, revealing images or text and highlighting images on the screen.

Lesson title	Objectives	What children should know	Cross-curricular links
Lesson 1: Body parts	**QCA Unit 1A** 'Ourselves' • To know that humans have bodies with similar parts. • To be able to name parts of the human body.	• The names of some body parts.	**English** PNS: Creating and shaping texts **PSHE** PoS (3e) Developing a healthy, safer lifestyle: Pupils should be taught the names of the main parts of the body.
Lesson 2: Animals and their young	**QCA Unit 1A** 'Ourselves' • To match young and adults of the same animal.	•That animals can grow.	**PSHE** PoS (3d) Developing a healthy, safer lifestyle: Pupils should learn about the process of growing from young to old and how people's needs change.
Lesson 3: Differences between humans	**QCA Unit 1A** 'Ourselves' • To know that there are differences between humans. • To collect and organise data (and present it in a chart).	• What the term 'humans' means. • How to compare.	**PSHE** PoS (4c) Developing good relationships and respecting the differences between people: To identify and respect the differences and similarities between people. **Speaking and listening** Objective 7: To take turns to speak, listen to others' suggestions and talk about what they are going to do, eg contributing in groups.
Lesson 4: How animals move	**QCA Unit 1A** 'Ourselves' • To know that animals, including humans, move. • To make observations and comparisons of the way animals move.	• The names of some animals. • How to compare.	**PE** QCA Unit 5 'Gymnastic activities (1)'
Lesson 5: Living and non-living	**QCA Unit 1A** 'Ourselves' • To understand that animals, including humans, are living. • To make observations of animals and use these to group them, explaining criteria chosen.	• How to make simple observations.	**Art and design** PoS (1a) To record from first-hand observation. **Speaking and listening** Objective 3: To ask and answer questions, make relevant contributions, offer suggestions and take turns, eg when devising ways of sorting items in the classroom.
Lesson 6: Plants all around us	**QCA Unit 1B** 'Growing plants' • To know that there are different plants in the immediate environment. • To treat growing plants with care. • To make careful observations of one or two plants and where they grow and to communicate these. • To know that plants have leaves, stems and flowers.	• How to identify a plant from a group of objects. • How to make simple observations.	**Speaking and listening** Objective 7: To take turns to speak, listen to others' suggestions, eg contributing in groups. **Art and design** PoS (1a) To record from first-hand observation. **Geography** PoS (2b) To use appropriate fieldwork techniques.

Lesson title	Objectives	What children should know	Cross-curricular links
Lesson 7: Plant parts	**QCA Unit 1B** 'Growing plants' • To know that plants have leaves, stems, flowers and roots. • To know that plants grow.	• How to make simple observations. • How to label a diagram.	**English** PNS: Creating and shaping texts
Lesson 8: Plants for food	**QCA Unit 1B** 'Growing plants' • To know that plants provide food for humans.	• That plants have stems, roots, leaves and flowers.	**Design and technology** PoS (5c) Design and make assignments using a range of materials, including food; (2f) Follow safe procedures for food safety and hygiene.
Lesson 9: Identifying and describing materials	**QCA Unit 1C** 'Sorting and using materials' • To know that every material has many properties which can be recognised using our senses and described using appropriate vocabulary. • To record observations of materials.	• About the five senses.	**English** PNS: Sentence structure and punctuation
Lesson 10: Grouping materials	**QCA Unit 1C** 'Sorting and using materials' • To know that there are many materials and these can be named and described.	• How to sort.	**Design and technology** PoS (2a) To select tools, techniques and materials for making their product from a range suggested by the teacher.
Lesson 11: Magnets	**QCA Unit 1C** 'Sorting and using materials' • To know that some materials are magnetic but most are not. • To think about which objects they expect to be attracted to a magnet. • To make observations, communicate what happened, and with help, use results to draw conclusions, saying whether their predictions were right.	• That some materials stick to a magnet and others don't. • How to make predictions.	**Design and technology** PoS (2a) To select tools, techniques and materials for making their product from a range suggested by the teacher.
Lesson 12: Materials for a purpose	**QCA Unit 1C** 'Sorting and using materials' • To understand that materials are chosen for specific purposes on the basis of their properties.	• The names of some everyday materials.	**Speaking and listening** Objective 11: To explain their views to others in a small group, and decide how to report the group's views to the class.
Lesson 13: Sources of light	**QCA Unit 1D** 'Light and dark' • To know that there are many sources of light. • To know that sources of light vary in brightness. • To observe and make comparisons of sources of light.	• Some sources of light.	**English** PNS: Creating and shaping texts

Lesson title	Objectives	What children should know	Cross-curricular links
Lesson 14: Sources of light at night	**QCA Unit 1D** 'Light and dark' • To know that sources of light show up best at night-time.	• Some sources of light.	**Art and design** PoS (1a) To record from first-hand observation, experience and imagination; (2b) To try out tools and techniques. **Religious education** PoS (3g) To know how and why celebrations are important in religion.
Lesson 15: Things that move	**QCA Unit 1E** 'Pushes and pulls' • To understand that there are many sorts of movement which can be described in many ways.	• That things can be moved in different ways. • How to make simple observations.	**PE** QCA Unit 5 'Gymnastic activities (1)'
Lesson 16: Pushing and pulling	**QCA Unit 1E** 'Pushes and pulls' • To understand that pushing or pulling things can make objects start or stop moving. • To identify similarities and differences between the movement of different objects. • To make suggestions about how objects can be made to move and to find out whether they were right.	• That things can be moved in different ways.	**Speaking and listening** Objective 3: To ask and answer questions, make relevant contributions, offer suggestions and take turns, eg when devising ways of sorting items in the classroom.
Lesson 17: What's making it move?	**QCA Unit 1E** 'Pushes and pulls' • To understand that it is not only ourselves that make things move by pushing. • To ask questions about what is causing movement.	• That things can be moved in different ways. • How to sort.	**Speaking and listening** Objective 3: To ask and answer questions, make relevant contributions, offer suggestions and take turns, eg when devising ways of sorting items in the classroom.
Lesson 18: Sounds around us	**QCA Unit 1F** 'Sound and hearing' • To know that there are many different sources of sounds. • To explore sounds using their sense of hearing. • To make observations of sounds by listening carefully.	• That hearing is one of the five senses. • That there are many different sounds. • That we hear things when sounds enter our ears.	**Speaking and listening** Objective 2: To listen with sustained concentration.
Lesson 19: Different ways of making sounds	**QCA Unit 1F** 'Sound and hearing' • To know that there are many different ways of making sounds. • To present results and to interpret these.	• That musical instruments can make different sounds. • That we hear things when sounds enter our ears.	**Music** QCA Unit 6 'Exploring instruments and symbols'
Lesson 20: Describing sounds	**QCA Unit 1F** 'Sound and hearing' • To know that there are many ways of describing sounds.	• That there are many different sounds. • That we hear things when sounds enter our ears.	**Speaking and listening** Objective 2: To listen with sustained concentration. **English** PNS: Sentence structure and punctuation **English** PNS: Creating and shaping texts

Body parts

Learning objectives
QCA Unit 1A 'Ourselves'
● To know that humans have bodies with similar parts.
● To be able to name parts of the human body.

Resources
'Body parts' Notebook file; photocopiable page 127 'Body parts', one for each child; sticky notes.

Links to other subjects
English
PNS: Creating and shaping texts
PSHE
PoS (3e) Developing a healthy, safer lifestyle: Pupils should be taught the names of the main parts of the body.
● Both these objectives link well with this lesson.

Starter
Open page 2 of the Notebook file and sing 'Head, Shoulders, Knees and Toes', ensuring that the children point to the correct body parts as they sing along. Ask them to tell you what the song is about. Introduce the phrase *body parts*.

Sing the song a second time, but this time tell the children not to say the word *head*, but just to touch their heads instead. For each verse thereafter, add another body part that the children should touch instead of saying the word out loud.

Whole-class shared work
● Go to page 3. Slowly move the Screen Shade to reveal the body part image, asking the children to identify it. Repeat this for pages 4 to 12, writing the name of the body part on each page.
● Go to page 13. Ask the children to help you write a list of body parts in preparation for their independent work.
● Play 'Simon Says', using the list of body parts.

Independent work
● Hand out copies of photocopiable page 127. Ask the children to label the body, choosing the appropriate word from the word bank at the bottom of the sheet.
● Less confident learners could be given sticky notes with the names of the body parts to stick onto themselves (or onto a large drawing of a child).
● Give more confident learners an adapted sheet with the word bank and/or arrows removed.

Plenary
● Enable the Spotlight tool, choose the circle and make it smaller. Go to page 14 of the Notebook file and move the spotlight around the image of the body, asking the children to name the body parts that they can identify.
● Write relevant words to label the body. Write any further labels that the children may suggest.
● Ensure that the children understand that these body parts are common to all humans.

Whiteboard tools
Use the Screen Shade to reveal images on the pages. Use the Spotlight tool to focus on specific areas of an image.

 Pen tray

 Select tool

 Screen Shade

 Spotlight tool

Animals and their young

Learning objective
QCA Unit 1A 'Ourselves'
● To match young and adults
of the same animal.

Resources
'Animals and their young'
Notebook file; photocopiable
page 128 'Animals and their
young', one for each child; toy
animals to represent the
images on the photocopiable
sheet; non-fiction books
showing young and adult of
the same animal.

Links to other subjects
PSHE
PoS (3d) Developing a healthy,
safer lifestyle: Pupils should
learn about the process of
growing from young to old and
how people's needs change.
● Link the work from this
lesson to this objective.

Starter
Open page 2 of the Notebook file and ask the children to identify the
animals. Ask: *Are there any animals that go together or are similar?*
Encourage the children to explain their thinking. Use the Delete button (or
select the Delete option from the dropdown menu) to remove the large cloud
at the top of the page to reveal the question: *Can you match the young and
adult of the same animal?* Invite volunteers to come to the whiteboard to
move the images to match the young and adult of each animal.

Whole-class shared work
● Go to page 3 and read the questions: *How are the adults and young the
same? How are the adults and young different?* Ask the children to
discuss and share ideas with a partner before sharing with the class.
Annotate the page with the main points.
● Repeat the activity on page 4.

Independent work
● Provide each child with a copy of photocopiable page 128. Ask the
children to match the young and adult of each animal by drawing a line to
link each pair. Encourage them to name each animal and describe how the
animals change as they grow.
● You may wish to provide non-fiction books showing photographs of young
and adult animals, to support the children.
● Give less confident learners some toy animals to match, before moving on
to matching the images on the photocopiable sheet. Focus on the more
obvious pairings before moving on to discuss the less obvious examples
(for example, tadpole/frog, caterpillar/butterfly).
● Encourage more confident learners to think of further animals. Ask them
to draw the young and adult versions.

Plenary
● Go to page 5 and ask for volunteers to match the animals with their
young, as they have done for their independent work.
● Ask the children what they have learned. Share and discuss their work,
ensuring that they have matched the young and adult of each animal
correctly. Have they learned the names of any new animals and their
young?
● Go to page 6 and ask: *How do animals change as they get older?* It may be
easier for children to think about how their own pets have changed, if
they have any. Write their ideas on the page.

Whiteboard tools
Use the Delete button to
reveal the hidden question on
page 2.

 Pen tray

 Select tool

 Delete button

Differences between humans

Learning objectives
QCA Unit 1A 'Ourselves'
● To know that there are differences between humans.
● To collect and organise data (and present it in a chart).

Resources
'Differences between humans' Notebook file; photographs of people cut from magazines; large sheets of paper with sorting circles drawn on them, for recording.

Links to other subjects
PSHE
PoS (4c) Developing good relationships and respecting the differences between people: To identify and respect the differences and similarities between people.
Speaking and listening
Objective 7: To take turns to speak, listen to others' suggestions and talk about what they are going to do, eg contributing in groups.
● This lesson links well with the two above objectives.

Starter
Display page 2 of the Notebook file and read the question: *How are these humans different?* Ask the children to discuss their ideas with a partner before sharing them with the class. Write these ideas on the page or circle them on the images.

Whole-class shared work
● Go to page 3, and read the question: *How are humans different?* Ask the children to suggest ways in which they are different to each other and make notes on the Notebook page. The children could physically sort themselves into groups using some of the criteria given – for example, age, boy/girl, hair colour or eye colour.
● Establish that humans can have both similarities and differences.
● Go to page 4. Ask the children to suggest different ways of sorting the people, explaining the criteria they have chosen. Move the images to regroup them. Press the Undo button until the page is reset to allow for sorting using different criteria.

Independent work
● Ask the children, in groups, to sort a selection of photographs of people according to their own criteria. Provide photographs cut from magazines and large sheets of paper with sorting circles drawn on them.
● Group less confident learners with more confident partners to facilitate discussion, or group them to work with the teacher or teaching assistant. Provide suggestions for the sorting criteria if necessary, and refer back to the ideas generated in the Starter activity.
● Encourage more confident learners to sort using criteria with two variables (for example, brown hair *and* straight hair).

Plenary
● Ask the children to show their findings and explain the criteria chosen for their groupings.
● Go back to page 4 and use their criteria to sort the people on that page. Add any new ideas to the list on page 3.
● Use page 5 to write up the children's conclusions about what they have found out or learned from their exploration.

Whiteboard tools
Use a Pen from the Pen tray to add text. Use the Undo button to erase any unsaved changes.

 Pen tray

 Select tool

 Undo button

How animals move

Learning objectives
QCA Unit 1A 'Ourselves'
● To know that animals, including humans, move.
● To make observations and comparisons of the way animals move.

Resources P
Photocopiable page 129 'How animals move', one for each child; digital camera; glue, scissors and pens; video clips of different animals moving; large 'sorting sheets' (pieces of paper divided into four sections).

Links to other subjects
PE
QCA Unit 5 'Gymnastic activities (1)'
● Use a PE lesson as the Starter to this lesson. Alternatively, have a PE lesson after this lesson, to mimic the actions of different animals.

Whiteboard tools
Use the Gallery to find images to add to the Notebook page. Use the Shapes tool to create a circle for the Plenary.

 Pen tray

 Select tool

 Gallery

 Shapes tool

Starter
A PE lesson could be used as a Starter for this lesson. Ask the children to find different ways of moving - for example, by jumping, sliding, hopping or rolling. Make a list of these different ways of moving to use back in the classroom. If a digital camera is available, take photographs of the different movements.

Whole-class shared work
● Open a blank Notebook page, and write up the different ways of moving that the children explored in the PE lesson. Show the digital photographs if you took any.
● Ask the children if any of the movements remind them of ways in which other animals move. Write the animals next to the movement words (or use pictures from the Gallery 📷).
● Ask the children if there are any other ways in which animals move that humans could not (for example, flying).
● Watch the video clips of different animals moving. Discuss the different ways the animals move, and which parts of the body they are using.
● Use pictures from the Gallery to promote discussion about how certain animals move and which parts of the body are being used. Annotate the pictures and highlight the parts of the body used.

Independent work
● Hand out copies of photocopiable page 129 along with the sorting sheets (large pieces of paper divided into four sections).
● Divide a blank Notebook page into four, like the sorting sheet, and into each section write a different movement heading: *Walk, Jump, Fly, Swim*. Talk about what kind of movement each word describes, and ask the children to label their sorting sheets in the same way.
● Ask the children, in pairs, to discuss how each animal on the sheet moves and then to cut out the pictures and stick them in the correct box on the sorting sheet.
● Invite less confident learners to put their animals in groups without sticking them down to begin with. Discuss their choices with them, and address any misunderstandings.
● Encourage more confident learners to think of further animals to draw in each box. Alternatively they could think of other ways of moving, and create additional groups of animals.

Plenary
● Draw a circle on a new Notebook page. Place some animal images around the circle.
● Ask individual children to drag two animals into the circle and describe how these two animals move in similar or different ways. Repeat with different animals.
● Ask the children what they have learned in this lesson.

Living and non-living

Learning objectives
QCA Unit 1A 'Ourselves'
● To understand that animals, including humans, are living.
● To make observations of animals and use these to group them explaining criteria chosen.

Resources
Photocopiable page 130 'Living and non-living', one for each child; a collection of living and non-living items; scissors; glue; large 'sorting sheets' (sheets of paper with a line drawn down the middle).

Links to other subjects
Art and design
PoS (1a) To record from first-hand observation.
● Take the children on a hunt around the school grounds for living and non-living things. They should make observational drawings of the items that they find.
Speaking and listening
Objective 3: To ask and answer questions, make relevant contributions, offer suggestions and take turns, eg when devising ways of sorting items in the classroom.
● Encourage children to discuss their choices with a partner in the independent work.

Starter
Show the children a range of living and non-living items. Ask them what makes these things different. Establish that some of the items are living and some are not. Ask the children to look out of the window and around the class for other living and non-living things. Discuss the fact that plants are living things things too – for example, trees and flowers.

Whole-class shared work
● Draw two circles on a new Notebook page and label them 'Living' and 'Non-living'. Add images of living and non-living things, taken from the Gallery (good folders to use include Mammals, Plants and Instruments), and ask the children to sort the images into the correct group by moving them to the relevant circle.
● Ask the children to explain why they selected 'living' or 'non-living' for each image.
● Ask them what is similar about the images in the 'living' set. (They are all animals or plants.)

Independent work
● Hand out copies of photocopiable page 130 along with the sorting sheets (large sheets of paper with a line drawn down the middle).
● Demonstrate how to label the sorting sheet by drawing it on the whiteboard, and filling in 'Living' and 'Non-living' as headings.
● Ask the children to discuss whether each item on the photocopiable sheet is living or non-living. They should then sort the images appropriately by cutting them out and sticking them into the relevant column of the sorting sheet.
● Ask the children to explain why they selected living or non-living for different items.
● Invite less confident learners to sort their items into two groups without sticking them down to begin with. Discuss their choices with them, and address any misunderstandings.
● Encourage more confident learners to think of further living or non-living items to draw in each column.

Plenary
● Ask the children to share and discuss their work.
● The work could be reproduced on the Notebook file using images from the Gallery. Each image could be put on a Notebook page and the children asked to finish a sentence written underneath, using the words *living* or *non-living*. For example: *The dog is ___* .
● Ask the children to explain what all living things have in common. (All living things can grow, move, reproduce, feed and breathe.) Write this definition on a Notebook page with some images of living things.

Whiteboard tools
Use the Shapes tool to create shapes. Use the Gallery to find images to add to the page.

 Pen tray

 Select tool

 Shapes tool

 Gallery

Plants all around us

Learning objectives
QCA Unit 1B 'Growing plants'
● To know that there are different plants in the immediate environment.
● To treat growing plants with care.
● To make careful observations of one or two plants and where they grow and to communicate these.
● To know that plants have leaves, stems and flowers.

Resources
'Plants all around us' Notebook file; a collection of real plants, including (if available) some of the following: daffodil, daisy, dandelion, grass, cactus, rose, holly, ivy, sunflower, tulip; clipboards, paper, labels and pencils; large outline of the school grounds for each group.

Links to other subjects
Speaking and listening
Objective 7: To take turns to speak, listen to others' suggestions, eg contributing in groups.
Art and design
PoS (1a) To record from first-hand observation.
● Both the above objectives link well with this lesson.
Geography
PoS (2b) To use appropriate fieldwork techniques.
● Encourage the children to record their information on a school plan as they carry out their plant hunt.

Starter
Open page 2 of the Notebook file. Ask the children to name the plants on the page. Check they are correct by using the Eraser from the Pen tray to erase the blue lines under each image. Show real examples of the plants, if available.

Move to page 3. Ask the children to name and describe any other plants they know, and write these on the page.

Whole-class shared work
● Go to page 4 and ask the children to suggest ways of grouping the plants. Move the plants around in accordance with their suggestions. Can they explain their criteria?
● Press the Undo button until the page is reset and ask the children to group the plants in a different way.

Independent work
● Take the children on a plant hunt around the school. Divide them into mixed-ability groups and give each group a large outline of the school grounds. They should use this to record the plants they find, showing where they found them.
● Ask them to look for plants growing in as many different places as they can. Ask: *Why do you think these plants are growing here?* Ask the children to name the main parts of the plants they find. They could make observational drawings of some of the plants.
● Ensure that less confident learners are supported by more confident learners, and are not left out of discussion and recording.
● On returning to the classroom, ask each group to share their findings, naming and describing the plants they found and stating where they were growing.
● Record the findings on page 5 of the Notebook file.

Plenary
● Ask the children what they have learned and make notes on page 6.
● Invite them to explain what all plants have in common. (Plants have similar parts, stem, roots, leaves and sometimes flowers.) This could be illustrated by labelling the plant displayed on page 7 and writing a definition.

Whiteboard tools
Use a Pen from the Pen tray to add text to the page. Use the Undo button to erase any unsaved changes.

 Pen tray

 Select tool

 Undo button

Plant parts

Starter

Remind the children of the previous lesson, when they looked for plants in the school grounds. Ask them to name some of the plants they found. Ask: *What did the different plants have in common?* (They all have leaves, roots, stems and sometimes flowers.)

Open the 'Build your own' file, which consists of a blank Notebook page and a ready-made Gallery collection of images located in My Content . Write the names of the plant parts on the first page. Ask the children to identify these plant parts on a real plant. (It may be useful to have a plant that needs re-potting, so that it can be removed from the pot to show its roots.)

Whole-class shared work

● Read or tell the story of 'Jack and the Beanstalk', using your prepared Notebook file showing the stages of development of a bean plant. When describing how the beanstalk grew, explain the growing process in detail, including the terms *roots, stem, leaves* and *flowers*.
● After telling the story, ask the children which plant parts were mentioned in the story.
● Using the Notebook image of the beanstalk, retell the part of the story which explains the growing process and point to each plant part as it is mentioned. (You will need to draw the roots of the beanstalk.) Label the main parts of the beanstalk.

Independent work

● Provide each child with a copy of photocopiable page 131. Encourage the children to discuss how each plant and its parts are both different and similar.
● Ask them to label the parts of each plant.
● Provide less confident learners with the words to label their plants, adding arrows pointing to each part.
● Encourage more confident learners to draw the label arrows where they decide they should go, and to spell the words independently.

Plenary

● Ask the children to share their work with a partner to check they have labelled the plants correctly.
● Ask them if they know of any other plant parts in addition to roots, leaves, stems and flowers. Write these on a Notebook page and, where possible, use images from the Gallery to illustrate these parts.
● Invite the children to share what they have learned in this lesson.

Learning objectives
QCA Unit 1B 'Growing plants'
● To know that plants have leaves, stems, flowers and roots.
● To know that plants grow.

Resources
'Build your own' file; photocopiable page 131 'Plant parts', one for each child; real plants, including one that needs re-potting; list of plant part words for less confident learners. Open the 'Build your own' file and prepare a Notebook file showing the stages of development of a bean plant, using the 'bean' images located in the Science folder under My Content.

Links to other subjects
English
PNS: Creating and shaping texts
● This lesson links well with this objective.

Whiteboard tools
Use the 'Build your own' file, which consists of a blank Notebook page and a collection of Gallery resources located in the My Content folder, to prepare a Notebook file (see Resources). Use the Spotlight tool to focus on different aspects of the beanstalk.

 Pen tray
 Spotlight tool
 Select tool
 Gallery

Plants for food

Learning objective
QCA Unit 1B 'Growing plants'
● To know that plants provide food for humans.

Resources
'Plants for food' Notebook file; photographs and real examples of plants that provide food for humans (for example, fruits, vegetables and cereals); recipe for vegetable soup, vegetable salad or fruit salad, and the ingredients and utensils to make it. (**NB:** Seek permission of parents or guardians before tasting food in class.)

Links to other subjects
Design and technology
PoS (5c) Design and make assignments using a range of materials, including food; (2f) Follow safe procedures for food safety and hygiene.
● Link the cooking activity with this objective.

Starter
Remind the children of any previous work on plant parts. Ask: *Why do we grow plants?* Write their suggestions on page 2 of the Notebook file. If the answer 'to provide food for humans' does not arise, show the children a photograph of a plant that provides food, such as a tomato plant or an apple tree. Ask them to suggest other plants that are grown to provide food for humans.

Go to page 3 of the Notebook file and invite the children to match up the food with the plants by selecting the images and dragging them to the appropriate position on the page.

Whole-class shared work
● Show the children some real examples of plants that are grown to provide humans with food. Allow them to explore these plants and discuss what they see, smell and feel. If possible, let them taste the edible parts. (**Safety note!** Check for allergies before doing this, such as wheat intolerance.)
● Ensure that the children know the names of the different plants and, where applicable, how they are prepared before eating. Discuss with them which part of each plant is eaten: root, stem, leaf, flower, fruit or seed.
● Look again at page 3 and discuss where each food item grows. Discuss any different food items that you've looked at and show the children where each of these food items grows.

Independent work
● One or two groups could make a vegetable salad, a fruit salad or a vegetable soup with the assistance of an adult. Discuss with the children which part of each plant is eaten, and how it is prepared for eating.
● Other children could draw pictures of the food that was used in the whole-class activity, and state which part of the plant is eaten.
● If possible, show children who are uncertain the whole plant in context: for example, show carrots being pulled from the ground, to illustrate that it is the root that we eat.
● More confident learners could consider some food plants that are harder to categorise: for example, tomatoes and cucumbers are fruits but are used like vegetables.

Plenary
● Go to page 4 of the Notebook file. Ask a volunteer to drag the pictures into the correct column. Encourage the children to add the names of any other plants they have been drawing or cooking with into the different groups. Can they explain how they know which part of the plant is eaten? Can they add further edible plants to the table?
● Go to page 5 and ask why it is important for humans to grow plants. Note down the children's responses.
● Ask the children what they have learned in this lesson and write their conclusions on page 6.

Whiteboard tools
Use a Pen from the Pen tray to add text to the Notebook pages.

 Pen tray

 Select tool

Identifying and describing materials

Learning objectives
QCA Unit 1C 'Sorting and using materials'
● To know that every material has many properties which can be recognised using our senses and described using appropriate vocabulary.
● To record observations of materials.

Resources
1dentifying and describing materials' Notebook file; photocopiable page 132 'Identifying and describing materials', one for each child; a variety of objects made from different materials including wood, metal, plastic, fabric, sand and glass; drinking glass, teddy bear, spanner.

Links to other subjects
English
PNS: Sentence structure and punctuation
● Encourage the children to write some riddles of their own, describing objects in simple sentences, for others to guess.

Starter
Display page 2 of the Notebook file. Ask the children to identify some of the objects on the page. Allow them to handle the real objects made from a variety of materials, asking and answering the questions on the page.

Go to page 3 and ask the children to name the types of materials the different objects were made from: wood, metal, plastic, fabric, sand and glass. Write these on the Notebook page. Ask the children to identify further examples of each material in the classroom.

Whole-class shared work
● Go to page 4 and read the questions. Using some of the objects from the Starter, ask the children to provide answers to the two questions. Write a list of suggested descriptive words on the Notebook page.
● Move to page 5. Using the list of common materials on page 3 and the descriptive words on page 4, ask the children to help you complete the sentences: *This is a* _____ (bottle). *It is made from* _____ (glass). *It is* _____ (transparent, smooth and breakable). You may wish to have a real bottle available for the children to examine.
● Pages 6 and 7 allow opportunities for further reinforcement of the descriptive activity. Page 6 shows an image of a glove and page 7 shows an image of a spoon. Again, it would be helpful if you could provide a real example of each item for the children to look at and hold.

Independent work
● Hand out copies of photocopiable page 132 and provide a range of objects made from different materials.
● Ask the children to choose three different objects and complete the sentences on the sheet for each object: *This is a* _____ . *It is made from* _____ . *It is* _____ (descriptive words).
● You may wish to display the materials words and the descriptive words provided by the children during the whole-class shared work, to support the children in their writing.
● Give less confident learners a word bank to draw from for their descriptive phrases. Encourage them to spend time looking at each object, and then to hold it and shut their eyes so that they can concentrate on what the object feels like.
● Encourage more confident learners to think of further, new words to describe the objects.

Plenary
● Open page 8 of the Notebook file. Read the descriptions of each object and ask the children to predict which kitchen object is hidden under the blue box (you may wish to have real examples or pictures of the items available for them to choose from). Select the box under each description and press the Delete button (or select the Delete option from the dropdown menu) to reveal the object.
● Repeat the activity on pages 9 and 10.
● Go to page 11 and ask the children what they have found out or learned from their explorations. Make notes on the Notebook page.

Whiteboard tools
Use a Pen from the Pen tray to add text to the page.

 Pen tray

 Select tool

 Delete button

Grouping materials

Learning objective
QCA Unit 1C 'Sorting and using materials'
● To know that there are many materials and these can be named and described.

Resources
'Grouping materials' Notebook file; a range of objects made from wood, metal, plastic, fabric and glass.

Links to other subjects
Design and technology
PoS (2a) To select tools, techniques and materials for making their product from a range suggested by the teacher.
● Extend the ideas introduced in this activity by challenging the children to make a waterproof hat.

Starter
Remind the children of previous work on identifying and describing materials. Go to page 2 and ask them to recall the names of the common materials that objects are made from: wood, metal, glass, fabric and plastic. Write their answers on the Notebook page. Ask the children to describe each material and give examples of objects made from it.

Go to page 3 and ask the children to sort the objects on the page according to the material they are made from.

Whole-class shared work
● Display page 4 and ask the children to identify objects within the kitchen that are made from wood, plastic, metal, glass and fabric. Ask for volunteers to circle the object in the same colour as the 'material' word at the bottom of the page.
● Ask the children to suggest other items that could be added to the Notebook file that would be made from each of the materials. These suggestions could be drawn on the page.

Independent work
● Working in pairs, ask the children to explore the classroom and find objects made from each of the common materials - wood, metal, plastic, fabric and glass.
● Invite them to record their findings either in the form of a simple table, by drawing the objects in groups and adding labels, or by sticking prepared written labels onto the items found within the classroom.
● You may want to set up some tables with a range of objects made from different materials for the children to sort into groups, as in the Starter activity.
● Encourage the children to describe the properties of the materials as they explore and sort.
● Pair less confident learners with a more confident partner to help guide their exploration and discussion.
● Challenge more confident learners to add some words to describe each material, using terms such as *hard, bendy, shiny* and so on.

Plenary
● Invite the children to share the objects they found that were made from each material.
● Go to page 5 and ask the children to discuss why different objects are made from different materials. Use examples from the independent work. For example: *Why are the sinks made from metal? Why are the pencils made from wood?*
● Go to page 6 and ask the children what they have learned today. Note down their responses on the Notebook page.

Whiteboard tools
Use a Pen from the Pen tray to add text.

 Pen tray

 Select tool

Magnets

Learning objectives
QCA Unit 1C 'Sorting and using materials'
● To know that some materials are magnetic but most are not.
● To think about which objects they expect to be attracted to a magnet.
● To make observations, communicate what happened, and with help, use results to draw conclusions saying whether their predictions were right.

Resources
'Build your own' file; a range of magnets, including bar magnets, horseshoe magnets, fridge magnets, magnetic alphabet letters; a range of magnetic and non-magnetic objects; sorting hoops; prepared recording sheets (two circles labelled 'magnetic' and 'non-magnetic') for each child. Open the 'Build your own' file, which consists of a blank Notebook page and a collection of Gallery resources, and add the picture of a magnet (located in the Science folder under My Content) to page 1. On page 2, draw two separate circles and label them 'magnetic' and non-magnetic'. Add a two-column grid with the same labels to page 3.

Links to other subjects
Design and technology
PoS (2a) To select tools, techniques and materials for making their product from a range suggested by the teacher.
● This activity could be extended to create a magnetic fishing game, by selecting and attaching pieces of magnetic materials to cardboard fish shapes.

Whiteboard tools

 Pen tray

 Select tool

 Shapes tool

 On-screen Keyboard

Starter
Show the children the picture of a magnet on the first page of the prepared Notebook file (see Resources). Ask them if they know what it is called and what it does. Write their ideas around the image of the magnet. Introduce the term *magnet*, explaining that some materials are magnetic and are attracted to a magnet, and some are not.

Whole-class shared work
● Show the children some real magnets – for example, fridge magnets, magnetic alphabet letters, or fishing games that use magnets. Ask them how they think the magnets work.
● Allow them to explore the different magnets and test them out on different objects and materials within the classroom, investigating which objects and materials are attracted to the magnets.
● Ask the children what they have found out about magnets so far, and write the answers on a Notebook page.
● Using the sorting hoops, invite them to sort some of the objects they have found into 'magnetic' or 'non-magnetic' groups.
● Go to page 2 to show the labelled circles. Draw objects within each hoop.

Independent work
● Provide the children with a range of magnetic and non-magnetic objects. Provide each child with a prepared recording sheet showing two circles labelled 'magnetic' and 'non-magnetic'.
● Ask the children to predict which objects will be attracted to a magnet and which will not, by sorting them into two groups and then recording their predictions on the prepared sheet. Encourage them to give reasons for their predictions.
● The children should then test their predictions using a magnet.
● Once they have done this, ask them to re-sort the objects and check their predictions against their results.
● Support less confident learners in identifying what each object they are testing is made from.
● Encourage more confident learners to suggest other objects that would belong to each group as a result of their findings.

Plenary
● Present the results of the exploration in the table on page 3 of the Notebook file, showing which objects are magnetic and which are not magnetic.
● Ask the children if they can see any similarities between the objects in each group. Ask: *Is the material from which the object is made important in predicting whether or not an object may be magnetic?*
● Invite the children to explain what they have learned about magnets. At this stage it is important that they do not think that all metals are magnetic. They should learn that iron is magnetic, but that other metals and other materials are not magnetic.

Materials for a purpose

Learning objective
QCA Unit 1C 'Sorting and using materials'
● To understand that materials are chosen for specific purposes on the basis of their properties.

Resources
'Build your own' file; photocopiable page 133 'Choosing materials', one for each child; wooden chair, metal hammer, plastic rain hat, woollen scarf.

Links to other subjects
Speaking and listening
Objective 11: To explain their views to others in a small group, and decide how to report the group's views to the class.
● Encourage the children to work together on the sheets, discussing what they are going to write, and how they will report back to the class.

Starter
Remind the children of previous work they have done on identifying, describing and grouping materials. Ask them to name some common materials (for example, wood, metal, plastic, fabric, glass and stone) and to describe the properties of each material. Display images of a range of objects made from different materials and ask the children to identify the material the object is made from and to give reasons why that material was used.

Whole-class shared work
● Ask the children to imagine that they are toy makers, and need to choose suitable materials to make different toys.
● Open the 'Build your own' file, which consists of a blank Notebook page and a ready-made Gallery collection of resources located in the My Content folder ⬚. Use the first Notebook page to display an image of a toy taken from the Science folder under My Content in the Gallery. Encourage the children to discuss what the material used to make that object should be like. Make a list of these properties.
● Write some common materials on the page. Using the list of properties, ask the children to choose which of the materials they think would be most suitable for making the toy. Tell them to discuss their ideas with a partner first and to give reasons for their thinking. Share ideas and circle the material they agree is most suitable.
● Using the same object, ask the children why the other materials would be unsuitable.
● Repeat this activity using different toy images from the Gallery, if further reinforcement is required.

Independent work
● Provide each child with a copy of photocopiable page 133. Ask the children to work in pairs to discuss which material would be most suitable for making each item, and to think of reasons why.
● Let them use the word bank at the bottom of the sheet, to help them complete the sentence for each object.
● Arrange for less confident learners to work with more confident partners. Ensure that the more confident child supports the less confident child and does not dominate.
● Encourage more confident learners to write more than one reason why their choice of material would be suitable. In preparation for the Plenary, they could write an unsuitable material for each object to be made from.

Plenary
● Invite the children to share and discuss their work, drawing conclusions about which material is most suitable for each object, and why.
● Show them real versions of each object, to confirm their conclusions.
● Ask them to suggest unsuitable materials for each object and give reasons why. Write their conclusions on a new Notebook page. Discuss which materials would be the most unsuitable, and why.
● Ask the children what they have learned during the lesson. Write down their conclusions on a blank Notebook page in the 'Build your own' file.

Whiteboard tools
Use a Pen from the Pen tray to write on the page. Use a Highlighter pen to highlight the best material in the whole-class shared work.

 Pen tray

 Select tool

 Highlighter pen

 Gallery

Sources of light

Learning objectives
QCA Unit 1D 'Light and dark'
● To know that there are many sources of light.
● To know that sources of light vary in brightness.
● To observe and make comparisons of sources of light.

Resources
'Sources of light' Notebook file; photocopiable page 134 'Light sources around the house', as homework for each child; story or poem about darkness and light (for example, *Can't You Sleep, Little Bear?* or *The Owl who was Afraid of the Dark*); torch, candle in a lantern, lamp, metal spoon, silver coin, foil or shiny paper, mirror; shopping catalogues; large sheets of paper.

Links to other subjects
English
PNS: Creating and shaping texts
● Extend the work in this lesson by asking the children to write some simple sentences describing light sources. These could be collected together as a class book.

Starter
Open page 2 and ask the children what they understand by the word *light*. Write their responses on the page. Display page 3 and ask them to identify objects within the classroom that are sources of light. Make a note of their suggestions. Discuss the different light sources with regard to whether the object gives out light, reflects it, or lets light pass through it.

Enable the Spotlight tool 🔦 and go to page 4. Use the spotlight to find light sources in the pictured classroom. Are any of these light sources in the children's own classroom?

Whole-class shared work
● Read a story or poem about darkness and light (see Resources). Ask the children to identify the light sources in the story or poem.
● Display page 5 and ask the class which objects on the page would make good light sources. Where relevant, link this activity to the poem or story. For example: *Which of these objects could have been used to light up the dark in Little Bear's cave?* Drag the objects that the children predict to be light sources (or not light sources) into the relevant columns.
● Test the predictions in a dark place or room. Ensure that the children can distinguish between objects that give out light and objects that reflect light. They should check their findings with the predictions they made. Discuss any misunderstandings.

Independent work
● Take the children on a 'light source' hunt around the school – for example, ceiling lights, computer monitor lights and motion detector lights. Ask them to draw and label as many light sources as they can.
● Using shop catalogues, cut out pictures of objects that would give out light (such as televisions, lamps, microwaves and so on).
● Working in groups, ask the children to create collages of light sources using the ideas and images from the above activities, and drawings of their own.
● Group less confident learners with more confident learners for the collage activity. If the concept needs reinforcement, provide them with some pictures of objects that do and do not give out light to sort into groups.
● Encourage more confident learners to think of objects that would not be found within the school or inside the catalogues, and make drawings of these – for example, illuminated shop signs, the moon or car headlamps.

Plenary
● Ask the children to show their light source collages. Encourage them to compare the light sources in terms of brightness.
● Display page 6 and ask the children what they have learned today.
● Provide each child with a copy of photocopiable page 134. Discuss the sheet, explaining to the children how to complete it, and give it as homework.

Whiteboard tools
Use the Spotlight tool to find different sources of light in the Starter activity.

 Pen tray

 Select tool

 Spotlight tool

Sources of light at night

Starter

Remind the children of previous work on light sources (see Lesson 13). Ask them why we need light sources and encourage them to talk about the times of day that we are most likely to use light sources. Can they think of times of the year when light is used as part of celebrations? (For example, Christmas lights, fireworks, birthday candles, fireworks, bonfires, Hallowe'en lanterns, lights at religious festivals.) Write or draw their suggestions on a Notebook page. Ask them to consider why many celebrations that use light take place at night.

Whole-class shared work

● Open you prepared Notebook file (see Resources). Display the image of a candle on a white background. Ask the children to compare how much brighter the candle appears when you change the background to represent night. (Do this by selecting Format, then Background Colour, and changing the colour to black.)
● You can repeat this idea using further light images – for example, a moon and a yellow star (search the Gallery for the images).
● Establish with the children that sources of light show up best at night, when it is dark.
● Ask them to help compile a list of light sources that would show up well in the dark (such as street lights, illuminated signs, fairy lights or the beam from a lighthouse). Write their ideas on a blank Notebook page.

Independent work

● Using the list compiled in the whole-class shared work, ask the children to create night-time pictures showing some of these light sources. They should use a wax resist technique, creating a drawing using wax crayons and then brushing over it with thin black paint to create a night-time effect.
● Encourage the children to compare how well their light source shows up before and after adding the night-time effect.

Plenary

● Invite the children to share their work and discuss what happened to the brightness of their light source when they added the night-time effect.
● Discuss which light sources would be the brightest.
● Ask the children what they have learned today. Write their ideas and suggestions on the whiteboard.

Things that move

Learning objective
QCA Unit 1E 'Pushes and pulls'
● To understand that there are many sorts of movement which can be described in many ways.

Resources
If possible, hold the Starter in the playground and make available large and small play equipment (for example, bicycle, skateboard, ball, skipping rope, frisbee, swingball game, toy cars, slides or swings); a few digital images of a local playground or park (copyright permitting).

Links to other subjects
PE
QCA Unit 5 'Gymnastic activities (1)'
● Follow up with a PE lesson in which the children demonstrate the movement words that were suggested during the science lesson. They should do this by performing short sequences of movements.

Starter
If possible, begin the lesson outside, looking at playground equipment and toys. Explore with the children how the items can be moved, and discuss with them ways of describing the movement.

Whole-class shared work
● Back in the classroom, display some images of toys that move on a Notebook page – for example, a swing, scooter, slide, bicycle or ball (copyright permitting).
● Invite the children to explain how each toy moves and to describe its movement. Write their suggestions on the Notebook page – for example, *swing, roll, go faster, turn*.
● Ask the children to think what the word *movement* means. Write their suggestions on a new Notebook page. Ensure that they understand that movement of an object can cause it to change position or direction, and to speed up or slow down. This can be explained with reference to the equipment and toys used in the Starter activity.
● Show your images of the local park or playground, and discuss how the various pieces of play equipment move.

Independent work
● Ask the children to draw a picture of a park or adventure playground showing things that move. They can include children playing with smaller items, such as balls and skipping ropes, as well as larger items such as slides and swings.
● Encourage them to describe the movement of each object to a partner as they draw their picture. They could label the moving objects with words or phrases that describe the movement.
● Less confident learners could work in pairs, or with the teacher or teaching assistant, or produce a drawing as a group.
● Encourage more confident learners to think of and draw further moving objects that could be added to their scene.

Plenary
● Ask the children to share their work with each other and compare the movements of different objects. Group items together depending on their movements – perhaps using actual images from the Gallery . Can the children think of other objects that move in similar ways to the objects in their pictures?
● Ask the children what they have learned today about movement. Write their comments on a blank Notebook page.

Whiteboard tools
Use the Gallery to find and add images to the page. Use a Pen from the Pen tray to write on the page.

 Pen tray

 Select tool

 Gallery

Pushing and pulling

Learning objectives
QCA Unit 1E 'Pushes and pulls'
● To understand that pushing or pulling things can make objects start or stop moving.
● To identify similarities and differences between the movement of different objects.
● To make suggestions about how objects can be made to move and to find out whether they were right.

Resources
'Pushing and pulling' Notebook file; photocopiable page 135 'Pushes and pulls around the house', as homework for each child; resources for modelling actions (for example, zip, roll of toilet paper, mobile phone, toaster, Christmas cracker, light switch and so on); objects that are moved or operated with a push or pull action; sticky notes or labels with the words 'push' and 'pull' written on them.

Links to other subjects
Speaking and listening
Objective 3: To ask and answer questions, make relevant contributions, offer suggestions and take turns, eg when devising ways of sorting items in the classroom.
● Encourage the children to work in pairs in a cooperative and supportive way, and to contribute to the class discussion, taking turns to speak and offering sensible suggestions.

Starter
Remind the children of any previous work on exploring different types of movement. Ask them how the toys pictured on page 2 of the Notebook file could be moved. They should demonstrate the actions and give reasons for their suggestions. Write the correct answers (*push* or *pull*) beneath each picture, ensuring that the children understand and know the difference between both forces.

Whole-class shared work
● Go to page 3 and read the question: *What other things do we push or pull?* Ask the children to discuss and share ideas with a partner. Write or draw their ideas on the page, encouraging them to demonstrate the force (push or pull) being used – where possible, with a real object.
● Go to page 4. Ask the children to sort the pictures located in the box at the bottom of the page into either push or pull actions by selecting a picture and dragging it to the appropriate side of the page.
● Model the force used on the different objects if you have any real versions of the items available.

Independent work
● Hand out 'push' and 'pull' sticky notes or labels.
● Ask the children, in pairs, to explore the classroom and place the *push* or *pull* labels on items that are moved or operated with either force. Encourage the children to discuss their actions when making the objects move or operate. You may want to set up a table with some specific objects for them to explore.
● Less confident learners should work with more confident partners. Encourage them to experience the pushing and pulling for themselves, so that they understand the difference between the two forces.
● Encourage more confident learners to find objects that are moved or operated by both a push and a pull action.

Plenary
● Go to page 5. Ask the children what they have found or learned from their exploration.
● Share findings for objects that were moved or operated by a pushing action and then for objects that were moved or operated by a pulling action. Ask: *Were there any objects that moved or operated by both a push and a pull?*
● Explain how the Venn diagram can be used to show the children's findings. Record a range of their findings using the Venn diagram on page 5.
● Hand out copies of photocopiable page 135 and explain to the children how to complete it for homework.

Whiteboard tools
Use a Pen from the Pen tray to add text.

 Pen tray

 Select tool

What's making it move?

Starter
Open page 2 of the Notebook file. Read the question: *How can things be moved?* Remind the children of previous work on exploring things that moved by being pushed or pulled (see Lesson 16) and write down some of these things. Point out that all these things are pushed or pulled by a person. Ask: *Can you think of anything else that might make something move?*

Go to page 3. Ask: *How could we make this boat move without touching it?* If possible, present this scenario with a toy boat in a large container of water. Write the children's suggestions on the page. Ask volunteers to demonstrate, and to identify the cause of motion: for example, blowing into the sails, pushing the boat along, or making waves in the water to move it.

Whole-class shared work
● Go to page 4. Ask the children to identify what could be moving in the picture, and suggest what could be causing the movement. Make a note of their suggestions.
● Repeat the above activity with the images on pages 5 to 8.
● Establish with the children that it is not only people that make things move by pushing – wind and water can also make things move.

Independent work
● Give the children a range of toys that are moved by wind or water.
● Ask them to explore how each toy moves, to describe the movement and to identify what causes it to move. Encourage them to ask each other questions about what is causing the movement.
● Less confident learners could be paired with a more confident partner to facilitate discussion, or grouped together to work with the teacher or teaching assistant, to guide their exploration.
● Encourage more confident learners to think about whether the wind and water are pushing or pulling the object.
● Ask the children to sort the toys into two categories: those that are moved by wind and those that are moved by water.

Plenary
● Discuss how the children sorted the toys, and compare results. Emphasise that these toys are not being pushed or pulled by a person.
● Go to page 9 and ask the children if they can think of any other things that are made to move by the wind or by water.
● Go to page 10. Ask the children what they have learned during the lesson, and record their conclusions on the Notebook page.

Science — Lesson 18

Sounds around us

Learning objectives
QCA Unit 1F 'Sound and hearing'
● To know that there are many different sources of sounds.
● To explore sounds using their sense of hearing.
● To make observations of sounds by listening carefully.

Resources
'Sounds around us' Notebook file; large outline plan of the school and its grounds for each group.

Links to other subjects
Speaking and listening
Objective 2: To listen with sustained concentration.
● This lesson links well with the above objective.

Whiteboard tools
Use a Pen from the Pen tray to write or add text to the page. Use the Eraser from the Pen tray to erase the boxes in the Plenary.

 Pen tray

 Select tool

Starter
Display page 2. Ask the children to recall the five senses and write them on the page (hearing, sight, touch, taste and smell). Invite them to identify which part of their body they use for each sense. Ask them which sense they would use for listening and then circle the relevant image on the page.
  Go to page 3. Ask the children to share sounds that they can describe and make - for example, laughing, clapping, whistling and other sound effects. Write some of the sounds on the board in one colour and words to describe them in a different colour.

Whole-class shared work
● Go to page 4. Tell the children to look at the picture of the kitchen and to imagine what sounds they might hear. Invite them to describe and imitate the sounds and identify the source. Press the different images to hear the linked sounds. Circle each sound source.
● Ask the children to suggest other sounds that might be heard in a kitchen. They could imitate or describe the sound to the rest of the class to see if the other children can identify it.
● Take the children on a listening walk around the school. Visit different areas within the school (for example, the office, another classroom, the library, the playground). Encourage the children to listen very carefully for different sounds.
● On returning to the classroom, ask them to recall the different sounds they heard in the different areas and identify the sources of the sounds.
● Write the children's findings on page 5 of the Notebook file.

Independent work
● Hand out copies of a large plan of the school and its grounds. Ask the children to work in groups to draw the sources of the sounds they heard in the different places on the listening walk.
● They could also add labels to identify or describe the sounds they heard.
● Encourage less confident learners to think of at least one sound and its source for each of the different areas of the school.
● Ask more confident learners to work in pairs or individually, and to use varied vocabulary when describing their sounds.

Plenary
● Ask the children questions about their sound maps. For example: *Which was the quietest or loudest place? Where did we hear lots of sounds? Which sound was the quietest?*
● Go to page 6 and play the listening game. Tell the children to close their eyes, and concentrate on listening. Press on the star above each picture and ask them to identify what is making the sound. Check to see if they are correct by rubbing out the question mark boxes using the Eraser from the Pen tray.
● Go to page 7. Ask the children what they have found out or learned in today's lesson, and use the page to record their comments.

124
100 SMART Board™ LESSONS · YEAR 1

Different ways of making sounds

Learning objectives
QCA Unit 1F 'Sound and hearing'
● To know that there are many different ways of making sounds.
● To present results and to interpret these.

Resources
'Making sounds' Notebook file; photocopiable page 136 'Sorting musical instruments', one for each child; a picture of an orchestra; a piece of orchestral music to play to the children; if possible, some orchestral instruments to show the children; a range of musical instruments that can be played by blowing, hitting, plucking and shaking, for the children to explore.

Links to other subjects
Music
QCA Unit 6 'Exploring instruments and symbols'
● This lesson links well to the above objective.

Starter
Remind the children of previous work on listening to the sounds in and around the school (see Lesson 18). Ask them to recall some of the sounds they heard and describe them using appropriate vocabulary – for example, *quiet, tapping, short.* Write their words on page 2 of the Notebook file, asking them to make sounds in the ways suggested.

Whole-class shared work
● Explain to the children that they will be investigating musical instruments to find different ways of making sounds.
● Open page 3 of the Notebook file. Press a star and identify which instrument is making the sound. Ask for volunteers to drag the image of the instrument next to the correct star. Repeat for each of the stars.
● Go to page 4. Explain that the different instruments make different sounds. Ask the children if they know the names of any of the instruments and write in some of these. Play a piece of orchestral music and tell the class to listen out for different instruments.
● Discuss the names of the instruments on page 5 and ask for volunteers to drag and drop the labels. If possible, have real examples of the instruments to show the children. Ask them to imitate or describe the sounds made by the instruments. Compare this with the sound made by a real instrument.
● Ask: *How do these instruments make their sounds: do you blow into them, hit them, pluck them, or shake them?*

Independent work
● Ask the children to explore a range of musical instruments, finding out how each instrument makes its sound.
● They should group the instruments according to how they are played – for example, blowing, hitting, plucking or shaking.
● Hand out copies of photocopiable page 136 for the children to record their findings.
● Allow less confident learners plenty of hands-on experience with the instruments, and discuss with them the different ways they are producing the sounds.
● Encourage more confident learners to label their drawings.

Plenary
● Go to page 6 of the Notebook file. Ask for volunteers to drag the images from the box at the foot of the page and drop them into the appropriate column in the table.
● Ask the children questions about their results. For example: *Which group includes the most or least instruments? Are there any instruments that could belong to two groups?*
● Ask the children what they have found out or learned from their exploration and record this on page 7 of the Notebook file.

Whiteboard tools
Use a Pen from the Pen tray to add text.

 Pen tray

 Select tool

Describing sounds

Learning objective
QCA Unit 1F 'Sound and hearing'
● To know that there are many ways of describing sounds.

Resources
Assorted recorded sound clips (copyright permitting). Prepare blank 'sound' books for each child: Make the back of the book from a piece of card. The pages of the book should be shorter than the card and stapled at the left, so that the top of the card sticks up above them. Each of the pages should be divided in two by a line. The top of the card should have two headings: 'Sounds I like' and 'Sounds I dislike'.

Links to other subjects
Speaking and listening
Objective 2: To listen with sustained concentration.
● Encourage children to listen carefully in the whole-class shared activity.
English
PNS: Sentence structure and punctuation
PNS: Creating and shaping texts
● Encourage the children to write short captions for the pictures in their sound books, identifying each sound and describing it.

Whiteboard tools
Use the On-screen Keyboard, accessed through the Pen tray or the SMART Board tools menu, to create separate text boxes in the Starter. Use the Gallery to find images or sounds to add to the page.

 Pen tray

 Select tool

 On-screen Keyboard

 Gallery

Starter
Remind the children of previous work on exploring sounds around us and exploring the different ways of making sounds. Ask them to recall some of the sounds from the previous two lessons. Type the suggestions on a new Notebook page, putting each one in a new text box. Ask the children to describe the sounds – for example, *loud, short, beeping, scraping.* Ask: *Which sounds do you like? Which do you dislike?* Sort the sound words into two groups: 'Sounds we like' and 'Sounds we don't like'.

Whole-class shared work
● Play some of your prepared sound clips (see Resources). Ask the children to listen to each sound, identify it and share their thoughts with a partner. Play the sound again, tell the children the source of the sound and then ask them to describe each sound. Write up their suggestions on a blank Notebook page.
● Using images from the Gallery 🖼, put up some pictures of things that make sounds, such as animals, vehicles, instruments and tools. Invite the children to imitate the sounds made by each object and to describe these sounds. Write up any new describing words.
● Ask the children which sounds they like, and which sounds they dislike.

Independent work
● Explain to the children that they are going to make books about the sounds they like and dislike.
● Give each child a prepared 'sound book' (see Resources).
● Ask the children to draw pictures of sounds they like and dislike on each page, under the correct heading, and to add a caption.
● Less confident learners could work with the teacher or teaching assistant to produce a group book rather than individual books.
● Encourage more confident learners to annotate their pictures with words that describe the sounds.

Plenary
● Ask the children to share their books with a partner.
● Invite them to describe some of the sounds they like. Are there any similarities in the descriptions? For example, *happy, funny, quiet.*
● Now ask them to describe some of the sounds they disliked. Are there any similarities in the descriptions? For example, *loud, banging, scary.*
● Ask the children what they have learned today. Write their comments on a blank Notebook page.

Body parts

◼ Label the parts of the human body.

▫ Use these words to help you.

arm	chest	nose	hand
ear	elbow	neck	mouth
eye	foot	toes	waist
head	hip	shoulder	leg
knee			

Animals and their young

▮ Draw lines to match each adult animal with its young.

Name _____

How animals move

◼ How do these animals move? Do they walk, jump, swim or fly?

☐ Cut them out and put them in the right boxes on your sorting sheet.

  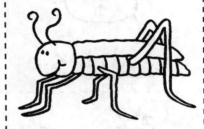

  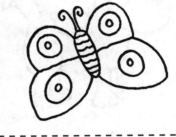

Living and non-living

- Which of these pictures show living things?
- Which of these pictures show non-living things?
- ☐ Cut them out and sort them into groups.

Illustrations © 2006, Jenny Tulip

Plant parts

◾ Label the different parts of these flowers.

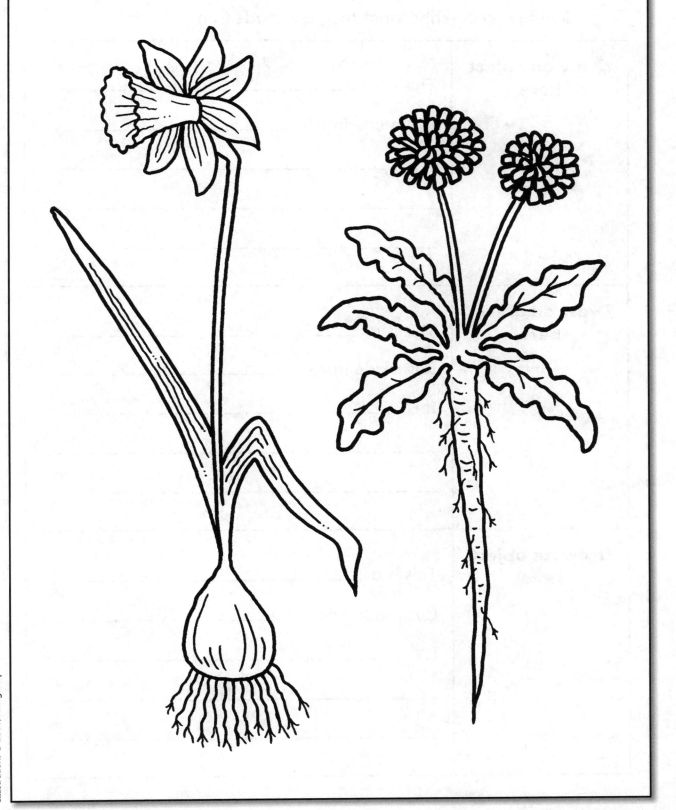

Identifying and describing materials

■ Choose three objects.

☐ Identify and describe what they are made from.

Draw an object here	This is a _____ It is made from _____ It is _____ _____ _____
Draw an object here	This is a _____ It is made from _____ It is _____ _____ _____
Draw an object here	This is a _____ It is made from _____ It is _____ _____ _____

Name _____

Choosing materials

■ Which materials would you make these objects from? Why?

The chair...	should be made from...	because it is...
The hammer...	should be made from...	because it is...
The rain hat...	should be made from...	because it is...
The scarf...	should be made from...	because it is...
The window...	should be made from...	because it is...

□ Use these words to help you.

Materials	Describing words
wood metal plastic glass fabric	hard strong shiny smooth soft bendy transparent waterproof

Light sources around the house

■ Find six **sources of light** in or around your house.

□ Draw them in the boxes.

Pushes and pulls around the house

◾ Find things in your house that are moved by pushing or pulling.

  ▢ Draw them in the boxes.

Things moved by pushing	Things moved by pulling

Sorting musical instruments

◼ Draw the musical instruments in the right boxes.

Blow	**Hit**
Pluck	**Shake**

◼SCHOLASTIC

www.scholastic.co.uk

Foundation subjects

This chapter provides 20 lessons based on objectives taken from the QCA Schemes of Work for the foundation subjects. The lessons cover a range of objectives from history, geography, religious education, design & technology, art & design and French. Interactive whiteboards are an ideal medium for helping young children to learn about the past. Large pictures, photographs, maps and websites can be displayed, making whole-class teaching easier. The range of tools available ensures that interactive whiteboards are more flexible than traditional teaching media.

Using hyperlinks to websites means that they can be accessed quickly and easily. Material can be prepared in advance, presented clearly and in an uncluttered way on a series of screens, and saved to be used again and again. It should also be remembered that annotated screens with notes can be saved to use in follow-up work, or to help refine files for use in the future.

Different learning styles are supported as text and graphics can be moved about the screen. The interactive whiteboard gives the class the opportunity to look at videos and pictures together, which can then be used as a stimulus for other activities, and video and sound files can be used. Teachers can act as scribes to annotate the pictures with children's suggestions, and the files can be saved for later review.

Lesson title	Objectives	What children should know	Cross-curricular links
History			
Lesson 1: Victorian houses	QCA Unit 2 'What were homes like a long time ago?' • To use evidence from photographs to identify similarities and differences between Victorian and modern houses.	• How to use artefacts, including pictures, to ask and answer questions about the past. • How to use time-related vocabulary, such as *before, after, long ago, year, old, new.*	English PNS: Sentence structure and punctuation ICT QCA Unit 1B 'Using a word bank' ICT QCA Unit 1A 'An introduction to modelling'
Lesson 2: Inside a Victorian home	QCA Unit 2 'What were homes like a long time ago?' • To identify objects found in Victorian homes and the differences between them and modern appliances.	• How to use artefacts, including pictures, to ask and answer questions about the past. • How to use time-related vocabulary, such as *before, after, long ago.*	ICT QCA Unit 1D 'Labelling and classifying' Science PoS Sc3 (1c) Recognise and name common types of material. English PNS: Sentence structure and punctuation
Lesson 3: Watch the birdie!	• To place events in chronological order. • To identify differences between ways of life at different times. • To ask and answer questions about the past.	• How to use artefacts, including pictures, to ask and answer questions about the past. • How to use time-related vocabulary, such as *before, after, long ago.*	English PNS: Sentence structure and punctuation ICT QCA Unit 1D 'Labelling and classifying'
Lesson 4: Toy detectives	QCA Unit 1 'How are our toys different from those in the past?' • To describe an artefact using everyday words and phrases. • How to decide whether an object is old or new. • To describe the characteristics of old and new objects.	• How to describe the characteristics of objects, for example in the classroom. • How to carry out sorting tasks. • How to look at old and new toys.	English PNS: Sentence structure and punctuation ICT QCA Unit 1D 'Labelling and classifying'

Lesson title	Objectives	What children should know	Cross-curricular links
Geography			
Lesson 5: Where I live ⬛P	QCA Unit 1 'Around our school - the local area' • To know their own addresses. • To understand what each line of the address means. • To be able to sequence features on a route.	• Where they live (this lesson is an opportunity to consolidate that knowledge). • About features they know in the local area, so that they can relate these to the maps.	**Mathematics** PNS: Handling data **ICT** PoS (1b) Pupils should be taught how to enter and store information in a variety of forms.
Lesson 6: Which way should I go? ⬛	QCA Unit 1 'Around our school - the local area' • To use geographical vocabulary. • To use maps and plans. • To use ICT.	• About plan views of common objects (for example, by looking at objects placed on an overhead projector, or digital photographs of objects taken from different angles).	**Mathematics** PNS: Understanding shape
Lesson 7: On our roads ⬛P	QCA Unit 2 'How can we make our local area safer?' • To use fieldwork to answer geographical questions. • To be able to suggest solutions to problems. • To be aware of the need to care for the environment. • To use ICT.	• How to tally – practise as a classroom-based activity (for example, favourite foods).	**Science** PoS Sc2 (5a) Find out about plants in the local environment. **English** PNS: Sentence structure and punctuation
Lesson 8: Far away places ⬛	QCA Unit 5 'Where in the world is Barnaby Bear?' • To observe and record. • To use geographical vocabulary. • To describe where places are.	• How to identify well-known countries and locations on a map. • How to complete simple matching activities on the whiteboard. • How to use a globe.	**English** PNS: Engaging with and responding to texts **ICT** PoS (3a) To share their ideas by presenting information in a variety of forms.
Design and technology			
Lesson 9: Fruit and vegetables ⬛ ⬛P	QCA Unit 1C 'Eat more fruit and vegetables' • To develop a sensory vocabulary. • To know that fruit and vegetables can be classified according to their sensory and other properties.	• How to handle, taste and smell foods and discuss opinions and observations.	**Science** QCA Unit 1A 'Ourselves' **Science** QCA Unit 1B 'Growing plants'
Lesson 10: Types of homes ⬛	QCA Unit 1D 'Homes' • That we live in many different types of homes. • The names of different buildings and the main features. • To observe carefully and draw simple shapes. • To be able to recognise and name basic mathematical shapes in the context of houses and homes.	• How to talk about their own homes.	**History** QCA Unit 2 'What were homes like a long time ago?' **English** PNS: Creating and shaping texts **Mathematics** PNS: Understanding shape **Geography** QCA Unit 1 'Around our school – the local area'
Lesson 11: Sliding pictures ⬛ ⬛P	QCA Unit 1A 'Moving pictures' • That simple sliding mechanisms can be used to create movement. • To use drawings to represent products. • To model their ideas in card and paper.	• How to use scissors safely.	**English** PNS: Creating and shaping texts
Lesson 12: Rotating pictures ⬛ ⬛P	QCA Unit 1A 'Moving pictures' • That simple levers and sliding mechanisms can be used to create movement. • That levers are used in products eg scissors, balances and moving books. • To use drawings to represent products. • To model their ideas in card and paper.	• How to draw simple pictures.	**English** PNS: Creating and shaping texts
Lesson 13: Making moving pictures ⬛ ⬛P	QCA Unit 1A 'Moving pictures' • That simple levers and sliding mechanisms can be used to create movement. • To make simple sliding and lever mechanisms. • To use tools safely. • To model their ideas in card and paper. • To make their design using appropriate techniques. • To evaluate their product by discussing how well it works in relation to the purpose.	• How to use scissors safely. • How to draw simple pictures. • How to tell a simple story or sequence of events.	**English** PNS: Creating and shaping texts

Lesson title	Objectives	What children should know	Cross-curricular links
Art and design			
Lesson 14: Shapes in art	• To learn about visual elements, such as shape, colour and pattern. • To look at the differences and similarities in the work of artists in different times and cultures.	• The names of shapes – for example, triangle, circle, square. • The names of colours.	**ICT** QCA Unit 1A 'An introduction to modelling' **English** PNS: Sentence structure and punctuation
Lesson 15: Drawing a landscape	**QCA Unit 2A** 'Picture this!' • To record from first-hand observation, experience and imagination, and explore ideas. • To try out tools and techniques and apply these to materials and processes.	• About working with different media.	**Geography** QCA Unit 1 'Around our school – the local area'
Lesson 16: Self-portraits	**QCA Unit 1A** 'Self-portrait' • To talk about the differences and similarities in the work of artists. • To understand the term *self-portrait*.	• How to express likes and dislikes, giving reasons.	**English** PNS: Sentence structure and punctuation
Religious education			
Lesson 17: The Nativity	**QCA Unit 1C** 'Celebrations: why do Christians give gifts at Christmas?' • To learn about the story of the birth of Jesus. • That the concepts of giving and receiving are important in Christianity. • That Christians believe that Jesus is God's gift to the world.	• That celebrations are important in many different religions.	**English** PNS: Sentence structure and punctuation
Lesson 18: Being special	• To learn about the idea of specialness. • To identify what matters to them and others.	• A few bible stories, and stories about people who are special to particular religions.	**PSHE** PoS (5b) To feel positive about themselves.
French			
Lesson 19: Greeting someone in French	• To say hello and goodbye in French. • To ask and answer questions about how they are.	• Where France is on a map. • That French people speak a different language.	**Speaking and listening** Objective 4: To explore familiar themes and characters through improvisation and role-play. **Design and technology** QCA Unit 1C 'Eat more fruit and vegetables'
Lesson 20: Counting in French	• To count to 10 in French.	• How to count to 20 in English.	**Mathematics** PNS: Counting and understanding number

Victorian houses

Learning objective
QCA Unit 2 'What were homes like a long time ago?'
● To use evidence from photographs to identify similarities and differences between Victorian and modern houses.

Resources
'Victorian houses' Notebook file; digital photographs of houses in the local area (check permissions first); map of the local area; computers with simple word processors. Prior to this lesson, organise a class walk around the local area to observe different styles of houses.

Links to other subjects
English
PNS: Sentence structure and punctuation
ICT
QCA Unit 1B 'Using a word bank'
● These objectives link well to the independent work.
ICT
QCA Unit 1A 'An introduction to modelling'
● Make simple drawings of Victorian stained glass panels, scan the drawings into a simple paint package and use the Fill Colour tool to colour the drawings.

Starter
Open page 2 of the Notebook file. Discuss the different houses the children saw on their walk around the local area, and show them the digital pictures of local houses. Ask: *Which houses are old? Which are more modern? How can you tell?* Note their responses. Press the hyperlink and find a local map. Show the children the locations of the houses.

Whole-class shared work
● Look at page 3 of the Notebook file. Ask whether the children think the house is old or new, and why. Note their suggestions, introducing new vocabulary as necessary (for example, *bay windows* and *gables*). Ask questions such as:
  ● *What is it built of?*
  ● *Is the house big or small? How do you know?*
  ● *Describe the windows/doors/roof.*
  ● *Can you see any decoration?*
  ● *Are there any chimneys? What are they for? What does that tell us about how the house was heated?*
  ● *Is there a garage?*
● Ask: *Are all Victorian houses the same?* Look at the Victorian house on page 4 and ask the children to identify similarities and differences between this house and the one on page 3.
● Repeat this process for the Victorian houses on pages 5 and 6. Discuss the features and annotate the pictures. Emphasise that some features are common to all, but other aspects are different.
● Repeat the questioning and annotation for the modern houses on pages 7 to 9.

Independent work
● Explain that the children will be using a word bank to write simple sentences to describe the features of the Victorian houses.
● Go to page 10 and ask the children to list any words that describe features of Victorian houses. Ensure they understand what they mean.
● Discuss what sort of sentences the children might write. Demonstrate how to use the word-processing program and how to insert pictures into documents. Tell the children they will need to use the keyboard to add words, as well as the word bank.
● Help less confident learners to use the keyboard and to compose the sentences.
● Challenge more confident learners to write several sentences and to work independently.

Plenary
● Discuss features that are common to most Victorian houses. Repeat for modern houses. Use the Spotlight tool to focus on parts of the digital photographs used in the lesson.
● Go to page 11. Ask the children if they can identify which house had each of the features shown on the page.
● Page 12 shows pictures of features inside the houses, in preparation for the next lesson. Invite the children to apply the skills learned in this lesson to decide whether these features belong to old or modern houses, and which feature is the odd one out.
● Page 13 offers teachers' notes to help to identify the different features of each of the houses shown in the Notebook file.

Whiteboard tools
Use the Spotlight tool to focus on different aspects of modern and Victorian houses.

 Pen tray

 Select tool

On-screen Keyboard

 Spotlight tool

Inside a Victorian home

Starter
Ask the children to tell you what they know about Victorian houses. Discuss when they were built, what building materials were used and how they were decorated. List these on the first page of your prepared Notebook file (see Resources). Ask: *Do you think the inside of homes in Victorian times would be the same or different from houses now? Why do you think that?* Tell the children that they are going to look at some pictures of Victorian domestic appliances and compare them with modern ones.

Whole-class shared work
● Show the pictures of the domestic appliances one at a time, and annotate them with the children's ideas.
● For each appliance, ask: *What was it used for? What materials is it made from? How do we know it is old?* (They are damaged/rusty/dented; they are not electric.) *Do the materials give any clues?*
● Ask: *How were the appliances operated?* Explain how each appliance worked.
● Ask: *What room was it used in?* Introduce appropriate vocabulary – for example, scullery, washhouse and parlour. Ask: *Why would a carpet beater have been used outside? What does this tell us about floor coverings?*
● Help the children to understand that in Victorian times, housework was carried out by servants in homes that could afford to employ them.
● Ask: *Do you think housework was an easy task in a Victorian home? Why not?* (Housework was much harder before electrical appliances.)
● Display the last page of your Notebook file, showing all the appliances, for reference during the independent work.

Independent work
● Give out copies of photocopiable page 160 and the printouts of the last page of your prepared Notebook file.
● Explain that the children should choose three appliances and draw careful pictures of them in the boxes on the photocopiable sheet.
● Read the text in each writing frame, and ask the children to suggest how they could continue each one. Encourage them to give as much detail as possible in their writing.
● Less confident learners could use a word processor with a word bank.
● Children who finish quickly could draw and write about three more Victorian appliances. Alternatively, they could draw and write about the modern equivalent appliances (for example, a vacuum cleaner rather than a carpet beater).

Plenary
● Choose one appliance and display it on the whiteboard. Ask who wrote about this appliance and invite a volunteer to show their picture and read what they have written about the appliance.
● Ask if anyone wrote something different about this appliance. By combining the ideas from different children, build up some detailed text and use the On-screen Keyboard 🖮 to enter this in the text box.
● Repeat this activity for the other appliances.

Watch the birdie!

Starter
Open page 2 of the Notebook file. Ask: *How can you tell whether a picture is old or recent?* With the children's help, make a list of the clues to look for when deciding whether a photograph is old or modern. For example, clothing and hair styles; modern or old-fashioned features, such as a car or a horse and cart; whether the poses are casual or formal.

Tell the children you want them to look for clues in some photographs you are going to show them, to decide whether they are old or modern. Remind them that a black and white photograph doesn't necessarily mean the picture was taken a long time ago, although a colour photo is more likely to be modern.

Whole-class shared work
● Go to page 3. Discuss the setting for the picture, and whether it is old or modern. Ask: *What event might be taking place? What is the role of the girl?*
● Move to page 4. Ask the children to decide in pairs whether the picture is old or modern, identifying clues. Encourage volunteers to mark the identifying clues on the Notebook page. Discuss the children's ideas, pointing out hairstyles, styles of clothes, accessories and jewellery, the fact that the photograph is in colour, and that it features the Millennium Bridge.
● Repeat the activity with the next three pictures on pages 5, 6 and 7.
● Go to page 8. Gradually move the Screen Shade 🖳 to reveal the picture from the right, so that only one person can be seen at a time. Ask the children to decide whether the picture is old or modern, basing their decision on evidence rather than guesswork.
● Repeat this activity on page 9.

Independent work
● Go to page 10 and explain the recording sheet. Ask the children to work in pairs. Give each pair copies of two or more photographs (depending upon ability), and a copy of page 10 each.
● The children should decide which photographs are old and which are modern, stick them in the correct column and complete the sentence underneath, giving reasons for their decision.

Plenary
● Open page 11. Ask for volunteers to come to the whiteboard to sort the photos into 'old' and 'modern', justifying their reasons. Encourage the children to use time-related vocabulary.
● When all the photographs have been sorted, ask: *Which photograph do you think is the oldest? Which photograph is the most recent?* Encourage the children to give reasons for their answers.
● Ask the children what they have learned in today's lesson. Record their conclusions on page 12.

Toy detectives

Learning objectives
QCA Unit 1 'How are our toys different from those in the past?'
● To describe an artefact using everyday words and phrases.
● How to decide whether an object is old or new.
● To describe the characteristics of old and new objects.

Resources ▣
Enlarged copies of photocopiable page 161 'Toy detectives', one for each pair of children; prepared Notebook file: Page 1 – showing photographs (copyright permitting) of old and new toys, including a teddy bear, a train set, wooden, metal and plastic toys and computerised toys; Page 2 – showing a snapshot of the photocopiable sheet (provided as a PDF on the CD), together with about eight pictures of old and new toys (different to those shown in page 1); printouts of the photographs on page 2 of the Notebook file (one set for each pair of children); glue; pencils.

Links to other subjects
English
PNS: Sentence structure and punctuation
ICT
QCA Unit 1D 'Labelling and classifying'
● Let the children use a simple word-processing package to write extended descriptions of toys.

Whiteboard tools
Use a Pen from the Pen tray to annotate areas of the pictures that indicate age.

 Pen tray

 On-screen Keyboard

 Select tool

Starter
Remind the children of work they have done on dating artefacts (see Lessons 2 and 3). Ask: *What sort of things did you look for?* (Condition, materials, purpose, age and so on.) List these on a Notebook page. Tell the children that they are going to look at pictures of some toys and think about their condition and the materials used to make them, before deciding whether the toys are old or new.

Whole-class shared work
● Look at the pictures of old and new toys on page 1 of your prepared Notebook file (see Resources). Ask:
  ● *What is this toy?*
  ● *Has it got any moving parts?*
  ● *Is it soft?*
  ● *What is it made of?*
  ● *Do you think it is old or new?*
  ● *Why do you think that?*
  ● *Do children play with toys like this now?*
● Mark and annotate the picture with the children's thoughts and observations – for example, circling or highlighting dents or scratches.
● Say that some kinds of toys have been popular for a long time (for example, teddy bears). It is the condition that gives obvious clues to the teddy bear's age.
● Look at pictures of some other toys that have been popular for generations, such as a toy train. This time, consider the clues given by the materials from which it is made.
● Look at pictures of the computerised toys. Explain that computerisation is a modern technology.
● Together, formulate a list of descriptive words that can be displayed to help the children during their independent work, sorting old and new toys.

Independent work
● Ask the children to work in pairs. Give each pair a set of pictures of old and new toys, and an enlarged copy of photocopiable page 161.
● Explain that the children should look for evidence to sort the toys into 'old' and 'new'. They should stick the picture under the correct heading on their sheet.
● Using the word list on the photocopiable sheet and the words from the whiteboard to help them, the children should write adjectives beside the toys that help to justify their decisions.
● Less confident learners should work with supportive partners, or with a teacher or teaching assistant.
● Ask more confident learners to write a short sentence beside each toy, justifying their decision.

Plenary
● Display page 2 of the prepared Notebook file, and ask for a volunteer to move one of the pictures into the correct column.
● Ask why he/she thought it belonged there. Does the rest of the class agree? Ask another child to come to the whiteboard and drag and drop appropriate adjectives beside the toy. Repeat for the other pictures.
● Discuss with the children which toys they found hardest to classify. Identify the reasons.

Where I live

Starter

Display the envelope addressed to the school (see Resources). Read each part of the address. Ask: *What does each part mean?* Ask the children to supply their addresses, and type up one or two. Ask: *Which part stays the same in each address? Why is this?* (Children at school in urban areas are likely to live in the same town; in rural areas they will all most likely be in the same county.)

Whole-class shared work

- Show a map of the school area. Read the place names that are labelled and mark any well-known features, such as shops and churches.
- Mark the place where each child lives and clearly label the school.
- Look at the dots on the map. Ask: *Who lives closest? Who lives furthest away?*
- Tally the number of children who live in each road/area. Ask: *Where does the largest number of children live? Where does the smallest number of children live? Is there any area where no children live? Why?*
- Use the Area Capture tool 🖼 to save the annotated map as a Notebook page, for use in other lessons. (**NB:** Annotating and saving the OS maps is only allowed if your school is part of the LEA OS Map Licensing Scheme.)
- Choose a place on the map where no child lives. Mark a route from a house in that area to the school. Describe the route. Mention the roads and landmarks that are passed.
- Ask a volunteer to describe his/her route from home to school. Assist in marking the route on the map. Use a Highlighter pen to highlight features that would help a person find their way.

Independent work

- Ask the children to describe their own route to school to a partner.
- Give each child a large sheet of paper and ask them to draw a map of their own route to school.
- Hand out copies of photocopiable page 162 so that the children can cut out appropriate buildings and icons to add to their map. Ask them to draw in any other things they usually see on their way.
- Less confident learners may need help in planning out their route.
- Encourage more confident learners to label as many of the places they pass as they can. They could be provided with a special 'local area' dictionary of place names. Some children may be able to include some items in plan view, although the majority will use pictorial representations.

Plenary

- Ask the children to share their home-to-school maps with their partners. Can they describe the routes and explain their drawing and labels?
- Display a series of pictures of the local area that would be seen along a particular route (the pictures should be out of order). The route should be one that most children will know.
- Invite a volunteer to sort the pictures into the correct order.

Learning objectives
QCA Unit 1 'Around our school – the local area'
- To know their own addresses.
- To understand what each line of the address means.
- To be able to sequence features on a route.

Resources 🅿
Photocopiable page 162 'Getting from home to school', one for each child; digital representation of an envelope addressed to the school (scan or mock-up); URL for a mapping website, such as the OS 'Get-a-map' website at **www.ordnancesurvey.co.uk/oswebsite/getamap**; a Notebook page showing digital images (copyright permitting) of places along a well-known local route (the images should be out of order); large sheets of paper; pencils.

Links to other subjects
Mathematics
PNS: Handling data
- Use the data from this activity to create simple charts.
ICT
PoS (1b) Pupils should be taught how to enter and store information in a variety of forms.
- Create a bar chart of who lives in what streets.

Whiteboard tools
Use the Area Capture tool to save the annotated map to a Notebook page.

 Pen tray

 Select tool

 Highlighter pen

 Area Capture tool

Which way should I go?

Learning objectives
QCA Unit 1 'Around our school
- the local area'
● To use geographical
vocabulary.
● To use maps and plans.
● To use ICT.

Resources 💿
'Which way should I go?'
Notebook file; printouts of
page 7 of the Notebook file (or
a similar simple map with
north/south and east/west
roads), one for each pair of
children; URL for a mapping
website, such as the OS 'Get-a-
map' website at **www.
ordnancesurvey.co.uk/
oswebsite/getmap** (NB:
annotating and saving OS
maps is only allowed if your
school is part of the LEA OS
Map Licensing Scheme.)

Links to other subjects
Mathematics
PNS: Understanding shape
● Ask the children to
comment on the shapes and
positions of the objects on the
maps. When they give
directions to each other, they
should include references to
right/left turns where relevant.

Starter
Open page 2 of the Notebook file to read the instructions, then go to page 3. Reveal the picture by moving the Screen Shade 🔲 from the right-hand side of the page. Ask: *What can you see in the picture? Where was this picture taken from?* Discuss ideas before revealing the last part of the picture, which shows the aeroplane's wing. Repeat the activity on page 4.

Move to page 5. Explain that one row shows things as they appear from the ground. The other row shows the same things as they might appear from high up in a hot air balloon. Ask: *Which is which?* Use the Delete button 🗙 (or select the Delete option from the dropdown menu) to remove the strips above each row to check whether the children are right. Invite volunteers to come to the whiteboard to move the objects so that the side view is next to the matching plan view.

Whole-class shared work
● Show the map and the key on page 6. Discuss why the items in the key are drawn in this way. Look at the roads and the river on the map.
● Demonstrate how to drag the features from the key onto the map. Put the tree in the middle of a road. Ask: *Is this a good place to put the tree?*
● Ask volunteers to add features to the map. Model comments on the placement of the features. For example: *You have put your tree near the river.* Encourage the children to make a comment about where they place their features.
● Go to page 7, study the map and read some of the labels. Explain that the compass rose shows the directions. Model a short journey and mark it on the map, describing the route using compass directions. You can add further features to the map by dragging and dropping the symbols at the bottom of the Notebook page.
● Ask volunteers to mark more routes, using different-coloured highlighters and describing the routes as they mark them.

Independent work
● Ask the children to work in pairs. Give each pair a printout of page 7 of the Notebook file. They should take turns to describe a route for their partner to mark onto the map using a coloured pencil. They should describe a starting point and say where they have travelled to by the end of the journey. They could also comment on the features they pass on the way.
● Give less confident learners oblique pictorial features, as they are easier to interpret.
● Challenge more confident learners to include diagonal roads and describe routes using all eight points on the compass.

Plenary
● Share the finished maps. Remind the children of the significance of the shapes on the map.
● Go to page 8. Ask the children what their local area might look like from the air. Look at an aerial or oblique photograph of the school. If this is not available, look at the locations on the Google Earth website (at **http:// earth.google.com**) or a similar mapping website.
● Encourage the children to identify features and to explain why they look as they do.

Whiteboard tools
Use a Highlighter pen to mark
routes on the simple map.

 Pen tray

 Select tool

 Highlighter pen

 Screen Shade

 Delete button

On our roads

Learning objectives
QCA Unit 2 'How can we make our local area safer?'
● To use fieldwork to answer geographical questions.
● To be able to suggest solutions to problems.
● To be aware of the need to care for the environment.
● To use ICT.

Resources 🅿
Photocopiable page 163 'Our traffic survey', one for each child; results of traffic survey undertaken by the children showing how many of various types of vehicle were seen on a local road; digital map of local area; Notebook file of uncompleted pictogram, to record results; digital photographs of the different types of vehicles (copyright permitting); a short video of the road (or a webcam of a road such as **www.abbeyroad.co.uk** – press on the 'Virtual visit' link). **NB:** Check the website's suitability and safety beforehand (last accessed 13/8/07).

Links to other subjects
Science
PoS Sc2 (5a) Find out about plants in the local environment.
● Carry out a survey of where plants or animals can be found in the school grounds.
English
PNS: Sentence structure and punctuation
● Write a simple report on the findings of the traffic survey, and how the road could be improved.

Whiteboard tools
Use images from the Gallery if digital photographs are unavailable.

 Pen tray

 On-screen Keyboard

 Select tool

 Gallery

Starter
Tell the children that they are going to find out how busy the local roads are, and to think about what this means to them. Ask: *Which local roads are busy?* If they cannot name the roads, encourage them to describe a road by saying what it is near and what they see when walking along it. Ask: *Which roads are not busy? Which do you prefer, busy or quiet roads? Why?*

Remind the children of the survey they carried out (see Resources). *Which road did you visit? What did you count? How did you record results?*

Whole-class shared work
● Show the children the location of the survey site on a digital map. Ask: *Was the road busy? What sorts of vehicle did you spot?*
● Display the Notebook page showing the uncompleted pictogram. Point out the vehicle pictures. Ask: *Which was the vehicle you spotted most of?*
● Tell the children that they are going to record their findings by dragging the correct numbers of vehicles for each vehicle type into a column. Then they can easily see which vehicles were recorded most, and which were recorded least.
● Invite volunteers to drag the pictures from the stack, and make a column of the correct number of each type of vehicle.
● Discuss what can be observed from the finished pictogram. Ask questions such as: *Which vehicles make most noise? Which make very little noise? Was the road noisy or quiet?*
● Evaluate the pictogram. Would the children like to change it in any way?

Independent work
● Provide each child with a copy of photocopiable page 163. Go through the sheet with the children and explain that they are going to use it to record four facts from the pictogram.
● Less confident learners may find it easier to have an enlarged version of the photocopiable sheet.
● Ask more confident learners to write a sentence to explain what they have drawn.

Plenary
● Discuss the children's answers to the questions. Then show the video (or webcam) of the road with the sound off. Discuss how busy the road is, and ask the children to make a note of particular vehicles and the number of vehicles there are. Ask: *How noisy do you think this road is?*
● Play the video or webcam again, with the sound on if applicable. Did the children comment on how busy the road was? Did they comment on particular vehicles, and how many of them there were? How many children made any reference to the noise that the vehicles were making? The answers to questions such as these should give an indication of how much the children have understood about the process of a survey and what this survey was intended to find out.

Learning objectives
QCA Unit 5 'Where in the world is Barnaby Bear?'
● To observe and record.
● To use geographical vocabulary.
● To describe where places are.

Resources
'Far away places' Notebook file; objects from other countries in the world, brought in by the children; television news items and newspaper cuttings about other countries in the world; an interactive globe that shows day and night (for example at **www.worldtime.com**); outline map of the world, one for each child.

Links to other subjects
English
PNS: Engaging with and responding to texts
● Add the locations of stories and poems from a range of different cultures/countries to the world map display.
ICT
PoS (3a) To share their ideas by presenting information in a variety of forms.
● Print out the finished world map to add to the children's record of achievement.

Whiteboard tools
Use the Delete button (or select the Delete option from the dropdown menu) to reveal the hidden labels on page 5.

 Pen tray

 Select tool

 On-screen Keyboard

 Delete button

Far away places

Starter
Open page 2 of the Notebook file. Explain to the children that they will be finding out about far away places around the world. Use your internet browser to view a globe which shows day and night and which can be turned. Orientate the globe so that the North Pole is at the top and rotate it. Ask: *What do you think this is showing you?* (The Earth turning.) Point to the British Isles and ask: *What is this place called?* Ask why some parts of the Earth are darker than others (day and night). Point to and name some of the other countries of the world.

Whole-class shared work
● Return to the Notebook file. Go to page 3 and ask: *Why is this map of the world not round?* (It has been flattened, so that all the countries can be seen at once.)
● Press the image of the orange on the right-hand side of the page. This will take you to a separate page that shows a flattened orange peel. Explain that this is what was done to the globe to make a flat map of the world.
● Return to page 3 and mark the school's location on the map with the X. Point out that, because the world is so large, the X needs to be placed on the country rather than on the specific location.
● Go to the map on page 4. Ask a volunteer to bring up their item from a far away place, explain what it is and decide on the category it falls into: postcard, letter, food/packaging, people (for example, photographs of family), gift (such as a souvenir) or newspaper cutting. Ask the child where it is from and locate the place on the world map. The child can then drag the relevant icon to the correct place on the map. Use the On-screen Keyboard to add text below the icon to explain what it represents.
● Repeat with the other items, discussing what the children know about the places. Consider distance, weather/climate and proximity to the equator or poles.

Independent work
● Leave the labelled world map on display.
● Provide each child with an outline map of the world. Ask the children to draw on it their favourite three items. If they contributed an item, encourage them to remember which item it was and to include it.
● Ask the children to look carefully at the map on the interactive board and, using it as a reference, to colour the seas on their outline map in blue. If some children find this difficult, provide them with a worksheet with the seas already shaded in.
● Mount a large map of the world on a display board. The children should fasten their 'far away' objects onto the map in the correct location.

Plenary
● Watch a video clip (or read a newspaper story) of a news item that happened somewhere else in the world. Discuss the places mentioned and find them on the world map. Encourage the children to use the names of the countries and to say whether they are far from, or near to, the school location.
● Display page 5 of the Notebook file. Ask the children what the names of the labelled countries are. Delete the red boxes to reveal the names to check if they are right. As each place name is uncovered, ask if anybody brought in an item from that place.

Fruit and vegetables

Learning objectives

QCA Unit 1C 'Eat more fruit and vegetables'

● To develop a sensory vocabulary.

● To know that fruit and vegetables can be classified according to their sensory and other properties.

Resources

'Build your own' file; photocopiable page 164 'Fruit and vegetables', one for each child; a range of fresh fruit and vegetables – wash and prepare samples to taste, reserve whole items to cut up in front of the children (**NB:** check for any allergies beforehand); canned fruit and vegetables; digital camera. Open the 'Build your own' file, which consists of a blank Notebook page and a collection of Gallery resources located in the My Content folder, to prepare a Noteboook file, and add pictures of fruit and vegetables from the Foundation folder under My Content the first page (include more than one copy of each item so that the foods can be grouped in different ways).

Links to other subjects
Science
QCA Unit 1A 'Ourselves'
● The children should understand that they were using their senses to find out about the foods. Discuss why it is good to eat fruits and vegetables.
Science
QCA Unit 1B 'Growing plants'
● Look at the plants that produce the fruits and vegetables.

Whiteboard tools
Use the Lines tool to create a pictogram in the Plenary.

 Pen tray

 Select tool

 Lines tool

 Gallery

Starter
Show the children a range of different fruits and vegetables. Ask them if they recognise any. Can they name them? If they don't know the name of a fruit or vegetable, ask them to guess before revealing the answer. Write labels for the fruit and vegetables.

Whole-class shared work
● Show the children the selection of fruit and vegetables (from the Foundation folder under My Content 📷) on the first page of your prepared Notebook file (see Resources). Ask: *How are these foods grown? Do they grow on trees? Are they grown in the ground?*
● Write these two headings on the Notebook page: 'Above ground' and 'In the ground'. Ask the children to help you to sort the pictures of fruit and vegetables into the two groups by dragging and dropping the images into the appropriate column. Discuss and ask questions as you do this: *Have you seen fruit and vegetables growing? Do you know anyone with a vegetable garden or fruit tree? How are these fruit and vegetables eaten? Do they need to be peeled first? Do they need to be cut into pieces, or can they be eaten whole?*
● Emphasise that whether the foods are grown above or below ground, it is always important to wash them properly first.
● Ask: *Do you know what these foods taste like?* Prompt the children to suggest words such as *sweet, sour, crunchy* or *squashy*. Write their suggestions on a new Notebook page.

Independent work
● Organise the children into groups of three or four. Give each group a sample of fruits and vegetables to taste, along with a sample of whole fruits and vegetables to touch and smell.
● Provide each child with a copy of photocopiable page 164. Ask them to describe what the foods taste, feel and smell like, and record their thoughts on the sheet. If possible, let them compare fresh and tinned versions of the foods, adding their preferences in the final column.
● Encourage the children to give reasons why they like or dislike a fruit or vegetable.
● Ask them to take pictures of the fruit and vegetables with a digital camera.
● Less confident learners may need support when choosing words to describe the fruit and vegetables.
● Ask more confident learners to write a sentence about each fruit and vegetable.

Plenary
● Ask the children to share their thoughts and opinions about the fruit and vegetables.
● On a new Notebook page, use the pictures of the fruit and vegetables to create a pictogram of the foods that the children liked the best. (Use the Lines tool ⬉ to build the pictogram.) Ask: *Which fruit or vegetable is the most popular? Which is the least popular? Why?*
● Discuss ways to make fruit and vegetables more interesting to eat. *Which fruit and vegetables could be combined to make them more interesting? How could they be combined?* (For example, in a salad, in a mixed-fruit juice, in a sandwich.)

Types of homes

Learning objectives
QCA Unit 1D 'Homes'
● That we live in many different types of homes.
● The names of different buildings and the main features.
● To observe carefully and draw simple shapes.
● To be able to recognise and name basic mathematical shapes in the context of houses and homes.

Resources
'Types of homes' Notebook file; individual whiteboards and pens; samples of wood, plastic, metal and so on, for the children to look at and feel. (**Safety note:** Make sure the samples have no sharp edges.)

Links to other subjects
History
QCA Unit 2 'What were homes like a long time ago?'
English
PNS: Creating and shaping texts
● This lesson links well to these objectives.
Mathematics
PNS: Understanding shape
● Count the features of different homes and discuss their shapes.
Geography
QCA Unit 1 'Around our school – the local area'
● Look at the features of different local buildings.

Starter
Open page 2 of the Notebook file. Ask the children what they know about different types of homes. Discuss any previous work on homes (in history, for example).

Whole-class shared work
● Work through pages 3 to 7 to look at the pictures of different types of homes. Emphasise the name of each type of home.
● Move to page 8. Invite volunteers to drag and drop the words to label the features of the house. Discuss each feature's shape and the material it is made from (press on the box in the bottom right corner to display a list of shape words).
● Discuss the different materials used to build the school, and why these materials were used. For example, glass is good for windows because you can see through it.
● Have some examples of the materials for the children to hold, and discuss their properties.
● Look at the homes on page 9. Ask: *Can you imagine living in these homes? Which would you prefer to live in?*

Independent work
● Ask the children to draw a picture of their home and to label the different features. Encourage a sense of proportion. Display a picture of a home in the Notebook file, and point out the position of the windows and doors.
● Less confident learners could trace around the outline of a home on the whiteboard. Use the Shapes tool 🖼 to add a white shape to cover the picture of the house, so that only the annotated lines are visible, showing the children the outline that they have just created.
● Invite more confident learners to write sentences about their homes. For example: *I live in a semi-detached house*. Encourage them to write about features that they like about their home.

Plenary
● Go to page 10 of the Notebook file. Share the children's drawings and establish that there are different types of homes but many have similar features (for example, windows and doors). Make notes on the whiteboard.
● Use a tally method to find out how many children live in each type of home. Make a bar chart on page 11 to present the results.
● As a follow-up to this lesson, organise a class walk around the local area and ask the children if they can recognise different types of homes. Encourage them to observe the shapes of different features of homes and the materials that they are made from.

Whiteboard tools
Use a Pen from the Pen tray to trace the outlines of homes.

 Pen tray

 Select tool

 Shapes tool

Sliding pictures

Learning objectives
QCA Unit 1A 'Moving pictures'
● That simple sliding mechanisms can be used to create movement.
● To use drawings to represent products.
● To model their ideas in card and paper.

Resources
'Moving pictures' Notebook file; photocopiable page 165 'Sliding picture', enlarged and copied onto card, one for each child; a collection of books and cards that have moving parts that rotate or move on a pivot; drawing materials; scissors.

Links to other subjects
English
PNS: Creating and shaping texts
● The children can write labels for their diagrams to show their ideas of how to make a sliding picture.

Starter
Open page 2 of the Notebook file. Show your collection of books and cards. For each product, demonstrate the moving part and ask the children to describe what it happening. Look at what the moving part is doing and ask the children how they think it works. Draw diagrams and make notes as required.

Whole-class shared work
● Display page 3. Ask the children what they think may happen if you pull the tab out.
● Pull the tab out and discuss what is happening. Ask the children how they think the mechanism is working.
● Drag the sliding tab to the side of the red square to reveal the whole of the sliding mechanism. Does it work as the children thought it did?
● Discuss the sliding tab. Ask: *What shape is it?* Look at the pull tab. *Is this a good shape to use?* Use the Shapes tool 🔲 to experiment with alternative shapes that could be used. Select ones suggested by the children and discuss their properties.
● Look around the room at other things that may have handles for pulling and pushing.
● Look at the pictures on the tab. *What order are they in?* Point out that the picture you see first is on the right and the picture you see last is on the left.
● Annotate this on the board to remind the children of the left and right positions.
● Discuss how they could make this work using card. Ask: *Would you be able to just have one piece of card on top of another? Would you have to stick anything together?*
● Go to page 4 and demonstrate how the children could make their sliding picture.
● Tell them that they will be experimenting with making their own sliding pictures.

Independent work
● Give each child an enlarged card copy of photocopiable page 165.
● Ask the children to draw some simple drawings on their sliding tabs, to create the moving pictures. Remind them that the first picture they will see in the window will be nearest to the pull tab and the last picture will be furthest away.
● With adult support, help the children to cut out the windows and push the sliding tabs into position.
● Less confident learners may need support in drawing, and in noting their observations.
● Encourage more confident learners to draw labelled diagrams to show what is happening.

Plenary
● Go to page 5 of the Notebook file. Invite the children to share their models.
● Talk about what they think worked and didn't work, recording their ideas with notes and drawings. Encourage them to give reasons for their answers.

Whiteboard tools
Write notes with a Pen from the Pen tray. Experiment with alternative pull tabs using the Shapes tool.

 Pen tray

 Select tool

 Shapes tool

Rotating pictures

Learning objectives
QCA Unit 1A 'Moving pictures'
● That simple levers and sliding mechanisms can be used to create movement.
● That levers are used in products eg scissors, balances and moving books.
● To use drawings to represent products.
● To model their ideas in card and paper.

Resources
'Moving pictures' Notebook file; photocopiable page 166 'Rotating picture' enlarged and copied onto card, one for each child (they will also need some extra card discs); a collection of books and cards that have moving parts that rotate or move on a pivot; butterfly clips; drawing materials.

Links to other subjects
English
PNS: Creating and shaping texts
● The children can write labels for their diagrams to show their ideas of how to make a rotating picture.

Starter
Open page 6 of the Notebook file. Show your collection of books or cards. Look at the moving parts. Ask: *How do these pictures work?* Make notes and draw diagrams on the page.

Whole-class shared work
● Go to page 7. Select the yellow circle and drag the green circle at the top of the box to rotate it. Ask: *What is happening? How is the mechanism working?*
● Drag the circle to the side of the page to reveal the whole of the rotating disc. Explain how the circle rotates around its central point, which is represented by a dot, and that only the part revealed in the window can be seen.
● Explain that the central point is the pivot. When the circle is rotated, it rotates around the pivotal point.
● Ask: *Will the view in the window change if the circle is placed in a different position behind the frame?*
● Centre the circle towards the edge of the frame, then press and drag to rotate it. Ask: *What happens?*
● If the circle is placed on one side of the frame, there is a lot of empty space in the window. Ask: *What could be done about this?* (Make the window smaller; have another circle.)
● Select the circle and choose the Clone option from the dropdown menu. Place the new circle on the opposite side of the window. Ask: *What effect does this have?*

Independent work
● Give each child an enlarged card copy of photocopiable page 166, butterfly clips and extra discs.
● Ask the children to draw simple drawings on their discs (remind them not to draw too close to the centre).
● With adult support, they should push the paper fastener through the X in the frame and through the X in the disc. Get them to rotate the disc to see how their picture changes.
● Encourage them to experiment with placing the disc in different positions; fastening the disc through different pivotal points; using different pictures and drawings.
● Less confident learners will need support in drawing and noting their observations.
● Challenge more confident learners to draw labelled diagrams to show the different ways that the moving picture can be put together.

Plenary
● Go to page 8 of the Notebook file. Invite the children to share their models.
● Talk about what worked and what didn't work. Encourage the children to give reasons for their answers. Use the Notebook page to make notes or drawings.

Whiteboard tools

 Pen tray

Select tool

Making moving pictures

Learning objectives
QCA Unit 1A 'Moving pictures'
● That simple levers and sliding mechanisms can be used to create movement.
● To make simple sliding and lever mechanisms.
● To use tools safely.
● To model their ideas in card and paper.
● To make their design using appropriate techniques.
● To evaluate their product by discussing how well it works in relation to the purpose.

Resources
'Moving pictures' Notebook file; enlarged card copies of photocopiable pages 165 'Sliding picture' and 166 'Rotating picture'; scissors; drawing materials; butterfly clips; individual whiteboards and pens.

Links to other subjects
English
PNS: Creating and shaping texts
● The children could make moving pictures to accompany short stories they have written for presentation during a suitable Literacy Hour session.

Starter
This lesson is based on building and evaluating a card that involves moving pictures. It can follow either Lesson 11 or Lesson 12.

Go to page 9 of the Notebook file. Remind the children of their work on moving pictures. Ask: *What kind of moving pictures have you looked at? What do these moving pictures do?* Make notes and draw diagrams as necessary.

Whole-class shared work
● Tell the children that you want them to design and make their own moving pictures.
● Go to page 10. Discuss possible ideas for moving pictures, encouraging the children to think creatively. Write their ideas on the board and draw diagrams to help them to visualise what the moving part will look like.
● Go to page 11. Think about how the moving pictures could be made. Again, make notes and draw diagrams of the children's ideas.
● Ideas for a rotating picture include: different weather symbols to show the weather; the foods the children like (the window could be positioned in the middle of a person); different actions to show movement (someone in different stages of walking, for example).
● Ideas for sliding pictures include: old and new toys; a plant growing in different stages.

Independent work
● Support the children in deciding on an idea for their moving pictures. They can discuss their ideas in small groups.
● Remind them of the order in which things need to be done. They will need to draw their design first before they copy it onto card. Give each child an enlarged card copy of one of the photocopiable sheets, depending on whether they are creating a rotating or sliding picture.
● As the children make their moving pictures, talk through what they are doing. Ask questions, such as: *How well is this working? What could you do to make it better?*
● Less confident learners may need support in designing their moving pictures. Talk about how they would like the moving picture to work.
● More confident learners will be able to adapt the template to suit their design.

Plenary
● Invite the children to demonstrate their moving pictures. Ask them to comment on their own and others' moving pictures. How well did the pictures work? What did they like? How could the designs be developed?
● Go to page 12 of the Notebook file. Ask the children to vote on how much they enjoyed making moving pictures. Encourage them to share the reasons for their answers. The opinion scale on page 12 allows the children to think about the degree to which they enjoyed the task.

Whiteboard tools

 Pen tray

 Select tool

Shapes in art

Learning objectives
● To learn about visual elements, such as shape, colour and pattern.
● To look at the differences and similarities in the work of artists in different times and cultures.

Resources
Drawing/art materials; website examples of paintings by Kandinsky and Mondrian (good examples are *Squares with Concentric Rings* and *Circles in a Circle* by Kandinsky, and *Broadway Boogie Woogie* and *Composition with Red, Yellow and Blue* by Mondrian). (**NB:** The artwork is subject to copyright and should not be copied without permission.)

Links to other subjects
ICT
QCA Unit 1A 'An introduction to modelling'
● Use a computer paint package to create the pictures.
English
PNS: Sentence structure and punctuation
● Encourage the children to write short captions, giving details about their pictures.

Whiteboard tools
Change a shape's transparency by selecting it and using the Transparency button. Upload scanned images by selecting Insert, then Picture File, and browsing to where you have saved the images.

 Pen tray

 Shapes tool

 Fill Colour tool

 Lines tool

 Transparency tool

Starter
Explain to the children that they are going to look at the work of two painters who used shapes in their artwork. Give a brief background of the two painters. Wassily Kandinsky was Russian and Piet Mondrian was Dutch. They were both born more than 100 years ago. At that time, most art represented real things. These artists wanted to use shapes and colour to try to express feelings and emotions. The resulting paintings are examples of 'abstract art'.

Whole-class shared work
● Display a Mondrian painting on the whiteboard. Discuss the colours used and ask the children what shapes they see. Annotate their responses.
● Invite the children to trace over shapes in the artwork.
● Ask questions about the painting: *What does the picture remind you of? What does it make you feel? How do you think the artist was feeling when he painted this picture?*
● Clear the screen by selecting Edit, then Clear Page. Repeat the activity with another Mondrian painting, and a couple of examples of works by Kandinsky.
● Ask: *How is Kandinsky similar to Mondrian? How is he different?* Discuss with the children the reasons for their answers.
● Ask: *Which painting do you like best?* Discuss the reasons for their answers.
● On a new Notebook page, create an abstract picture using shapes (with or without outlines) and lines. Vary the thickness of the lines and experiment with different colours. Use the Transparency button 🔘 to alter the transparency of shapes.
● Invite the children to add one shape at a time to create a class abstract picture.

Independent work
● Ask the children to create their own abstract pictures using the art materials provided. Encourage them to think about what they want to do. Will they use lots of different shapes? Or a single shape in different sizes?
● Less confident learners could use stencils to draw their shapes, or just use lines and primary colours, in the style of Mondrian. With adult support, allow small groups of children to experiment on the whiteboard before drawing directly onto paper.
● Encourage more confident learners to experiment with the effect of putting different colours next to each other.
● Scan some of the children's artwork for discussion during the Plenary.

Plenary
● Display the children's scanned artwork on the whiteboard.
● Invite feedback, encouraging positive comments. Ask the children to say something they like about each picture. Annotate the pictures with notes about good techniques, or pleasing uses of shape or colour.
● Save the digital images as a record of the children's achievements. The pictures could be used to create a class calendar for the children to take home.

Drawing a landscape

Learning objectives
QCA Unit 2A 'Picture this!'
● To record from first-hand observation, experience and imagination, and explore ideas.
● To try out tools and techniques and apply these to materials and processes.

Resources
'Landscape' Notebook file; drawing/art materials.

Links to other subjects
Geography
QCA Unit 1 'Around our school – the local area'
● Draw a local landscape. Include several different features and describe them.

Starter
Tell the children that they will be creating a landscape scene. Explain that a landscape is a picture of a place. Go to page 2 of the Notebook file. Discuss the photograph. Ask questions such as: *Is this landscape in the countryside or the town? What is the weather like? How does the landscape make you feel? Do you like this landscape?* Discuss colours and shapes in the picture, and point out that things far away look smaller than things closer in.

Now go to page 3 and carry out the same activity. Reinforce the concept that things appear smaller as they get further away.

Whole-class shared work
● Tell the children that landscape artists used to paint their pictures indoors. Then, over 100 years ago, a group of artists called the impressionists decided to paint their pictures outside instead. (The French term for this style of painting is 'plein air'.) Ask the children whether they would prefer to paint pictures outside or indoors, and why.
● Display page 4. Discuss the painting, thinking particularly about the colours used, the simple shapes of the sails, and the way the trees get smaller as they recede into the distance. Trace round a sail on one of the boats, to show how it is a simple triangle.
● Use page 5 to encourage the children to create their own landscape using elements on the screen. Ask them to think about where to position the elements and size them, so that things that are far away look smaller.
● Point out that the elements of the picture are based on simple shapes: triangles, squares, and circles.
● Use page 6 to model how to draw a landscape. A semi-transparent shape has been placed over the picture (created using the elements on page 5). Trace over the lines as follows:
  ● start with the main part of the landscape (the large hills in the middle ground);
  ● next, add the smaller hills in the background;
  ● draw other natural details (the trees and the lake), followed by the man-made (human) features (the buildings and the boats);
  ● finish with the clouds in the sky.

Independent work
● Give the children an opportunity to create their own 'plein air' pictures. Ideally, arrange for them to work outside, drawing from observation using a range of materials. If this is not possible, they could draw the view from a window, or copy one of the photographs on pages 2 or 3 of the Notebook file.
● Encourage the children to think about the shapes of the objects they are drawing, and their colours. Remind them that far away objects appear smaller.
● Children who need more practice in pencil control could trace round objects and shapes found in landscapes in the Notebook file.
● Invite more confident learners to add detail to their landscapes.

Plenary
● Let the children share and compare their completed pictures. Scan in some good examples of their artwork and display them on page 7 of the Notebook file to look in more detail at the shapes and colours used.
● The children could also use images in the Gallery in subsequent sessions to practise building up scenes and experimenting with sizes of objects to understand perspective.

Whiteboard tools
Upload scanned images by selecting Insert, then Picture file, and browsing to where you have saved the images. Use images from the Gallery to experiment with creating different scenes.

 Pen tray

 Select tool

 Delete button

 Gallery

Self-portraits

Starter
Go to page 2 of the Notebook file. Ask: *What is a portrait?* Explain that it is a picture of a person's face. Now ask: *What is a self-portrait?* Explain that it is a picture that an artist makes of himself or herself. Look at some different examples of self-portraits from the internet (see Resources for suggested websites). Ask questions such as: *What is the artist wearing? What colours are used? What does the self-portrait tell us about the artist? Are there any interesting clues? How does the portrait make you feel about the artist?*

Whole-class shared work
● Look again at page 2. Ask a volunteer to come to the whiteboard and trace around the features. Discuss the proportions of the facial features.
● Go to page 3. Ask the children to 'build' a face as follows, using the elements provided:
  ● Start off by moving the different elements to one side of the page so that the children can focus on one face shape (the eyes, mouths and eyebrows on each face are all movable).
  ● Encourage the children to experiment with different combinations of features, resizing and repositioning them, and filling them with different colours.
  ● Discuss proportion, and how different colours and expressions convey different moods and feelings.
  ● Experiment with different background colours, and include different objects.
  ● Talk about conveying feelings through colour and facial expression.
● Press the box in the bottom right corner of the page to read some additional hints that the children might find useful when planning their portrait.

Independent work
● Tell the children they are going to make a self-portrait. Ask them if they want to use a mirror, or work from imagination. Discuss which method the children prefer, and why.
● Provide drawing materials and mirrors, and let the children draw a self-portrait. Encourage them to include a few objects that are important to them. Leave it up them how they include these objects.
● Less confident learners could work in pairs. They could take it in turns to stand in front of the whiteboard, while the other draws round the shadow cast by the head. They can then draw in features together, and colour the portrait.
● Encourage more confident learners to be experimental in their approach.

Plenary
● Invite the children to share their artwork and to comment on each other's work. Encourage them to talk about how and why they chose a particular way to draw their self-portrait.
● Go to page 4 and scan some of the children's artwork from the independent activity onto the page. Encourage the children to consider the question: *What does your self-portrait say about you?* Make notes of their responses on the Notebook page.

The Nativity

Learning objectives
QCA Unit 1C 'Celebrations: why do Christians give gifts at Christmas?'
● To learn about the story of the birth of Jesus.
● That the concepts of giving and receiving are important in Christianity.

Resources
'The Nativity' Notebook file; photocopiable page 167 'The Nativity', one for each child; children's bible with story of the Nativity; drawing materials.

Links to other subjects
English
PNS: Sentence structure and punctuation
● The children will be writing extended captions to their drawings in their explanations of their choice of gift.

Starter
Open page 2 of the Notebook file. Ask the children what they know about Christmas. Ask: *What do people do at Christmas? What food do they eat? Who visits them? Where do they go? Why do people celebrate Christmas?* Create a spider diagram on page 2 to illustrate the children's ideas.

Whole-class shared work
● Tell the children that Christians celebrate the birth of Jesus at Christmas time, and that the special time of Jesus' birth is also called the Nativity.
● Read the story of the Nativity from a children's bible, and include the wise men's visit to Jesus after his birth.
● Go to page 3 and press the thumbnail image to open 'The Nativity' sequencing activity. Ask the children to look carefully at the pictures and to help you to put them into the correct order.
● Discuss each picture and ask the children how it fits in with the story of the Nativity.
● Use the Area Capture tool 🔲 to capture each individual image in the completed sequence and place it on page 4 of the Notebook file.
● Go back to page 3 and press the red circle to select appropriate sentences to accompany each picture. These sentences can be dragged to page 4 via the Page Sorter 🔲 and used as captions for the pictures.
● Move on to page 5. Discuss the role of the three wise men. Ask: *What gifts did they bring?* (Gold, frankincense and myrrh.)
● Tell the children that the wise men gave Jesus gifts for a king because they believed He was a special person.
● Go to page 6. Ask the children if they have received gifts that are special to them, or gifts that made them feel special. Make a note of their experiences.

Independent work
● Ask the children what they would give to Jesus. Give them time to talk in pairs about what they would give as a gift.
● Provide each child with a copy of photocopiable page 167. Ask the children to draw their gift and to write a sentence to say what it is and why they chose it.
● Remind them that a gift does not need to be big or expensive. Some gifts cost nothing but can make a person very happy.
● Give less confident learners more adult support in discussing their chosen gift.
● More confident learners may be able to write a few more sentences about their gift.

Plenary
● Scan in some good examples of the children's work and add the images to page 7.
● Invite the children to share ideas and make notes. Ask: *Would you like to receive these gifts? Have any of you had the same idea?*
● End the lesson by telling the children that Christians believe that Jesus is God's gift to the world. He is a gift because He is a special person with special qualities.

Whiteboard tools
Use the Area Capture tool to take a snapshot of the completed Nativity sequence. Upload scanned images by selecting Insert, then Picture File, and browsing to where you have saved the images.

 Pen tray

 Select tool

 Area Capture tool

 Page Sorter

Learning objectives
● To learn about the idea of specialness.
● To identify what matters to them and others.

Resources
A story about a special person, to read to the children; large sheets of paper; prepared Notebook file: type separate text boxes listing special qualities - for example, *kind to animals, cares about the environment, always cheerful, helpful, friendly*; same captions written on card strips, one set for each team.

Links to other subjects
PSHE
PoS (5b) To feel positive about themselves.
● Remind the children about the special things that they see in others and that they are special too. Encourage them to think about the special qualities that they can develop in themselves.

Being special

Starter
Remind the children of some of the stories they might have heard about special people. Read them a story - for example, the story of Zachaeus the tax collector, which highlights the fact that Jesus made friends with people that others would not have anything to do with.

Whole-class shared work
● Talk about why the children think the person in the story is special. Refer to other stories that they may know.
● Discuss special people. Ask the children if they have someone who is special to them. In pairs, give them a few minutes to tell their partner who this person is and why he or she is special.
● Discuss what qualities make someone special. Show the children your prepared Notebook page (see Resources). Read the special qualities out loud and talk about what they mean. Do the special people that the children chose share these qualities?
● Invite the children to share other reasons why their special person is special. Add any further suggestions to the Notebook page.
● Ask the children whether they think we are all special in our own way. Discuss their responses. Encourage them by pointing out special qualities that they have.

Independent work
● In mixed-ability teams of four, ask the children to sort the card strips you have prepared into order of importance. Explain that they must help each other, and talk about why they think some qualities are more important than others.
● When the children have decided their order, they should stick the strips onto a large sheet of paper.
● Remind the children that they will be expected to talk about the choices they have made in the Plenary.

Plenary
● Ask a representative from each team to hold up their sheet of paper. Discuss the order in which each team has placed the strips. Ask: *Are there any similarities? Are there any differences?*
● As a class, discuss and order the text boxes on the Notebook page.
● Ask the children which qualities they think their friends have.
● Encourage each child to tell the person next to them which special qualities they have.

Whiteboard tools
Use the On-screen Keyboard, accessed through the Pen tray or the SMART Board tools menu, to type the captions on the Notebook page.

 Pen tray

 On-screen Keyboard

 Select tool

Greeting someone in French

Learning objectives
● To say hello and goodbye in French.
● To ask and answer questions about how they are.

Resources
'French' Notebook file; photocopiable page 168 'Greeting someone in French', one for each pair.

Links to other subjects
Speaking and listening
Objective 4: To explore familiar themes and characters through improvisation and role play.
● Link this lesson to other role-play activities, perhaps exploring characters in a well-known story.
Design and technology
QCA Unit 1C 'Eat more fruit and vegetables'
● Teach the children the names of more fruit and vegetables, both in English and in French.

Starter
Say *Hello* to the children and invite them to respond to you. Ask them for other spoken greetings (for example, *Good afternoon*) and gestures of greeting, such as waving or shaking hands. Make notes on page 2 of the Notebook file. If a microphone is available, use Windows® Sound Recorder to record some of the children's greetings.

Whole-class shared work
● Go to page 3. Ask the children if they know where the UK is, and circle it on the on-screen map.
● Point to France. Ask: *What country is this?* Say it is France, and that people there speak in French.
● Introduce Megan and read out the words in the speech bubble. Explain that she is saying, *Hello! I am called Megan.* With the children, recite *Bonjour* and *Je m'appelle*, which mean *Hello* and *I am called*, respectively. Invite the children to say to a partner, *Bonjour! Je m'appelle…* followed by their name.
● Move to page 4. Tell the class that *Bonjour! Comment t'appelle tu?* is French for *Hello, what are you called?* Invite volunteers to reply with *Bonjour! Je m'appelle…* followed by their name.
● Go to page 5. Explain that *Ça va?* is French for *Are you well?*, and that the response *Ça va bien, merci!* means *I am well, thank you!* Invite the children to practise the exchange.
● Display page 6. Discuss what is happening in each of the pictures. Explain that many French people kiss each other on both cheeks when they meet.
● Tell the children they are going to role play the two characters. Make sure they are confident about the French words they have to say.

Independent work
● Group the children in pairs. Give each pair a copy of photocopiable page 168. Allow time for the children to practise the role play displayed on the sheet.
● Work with less confident learners, making sure that they can say the French phrases confidently. Restrict them to the first two pictures if necessary.
● Encourage more confident learners to work out another role play, in which they ask each other their names. (*Comment t'appelle tu? Je m'appelle…*)

Plenary
● Ask the different pairs of children to perform the role play. You may wish to record or film their performances.
● Praise the children in French – for example, *C'est bon! Magnifique! Très bien!*
● Ask the rest of the class for their feedback.

Whiteboard tools
If a microphone is available, use Windows® Sound Recorder (accessed through Start>Programs>Accessories>Entertainment) to record some of the children's greetings in the Starter.

 Pen tray

 Select tool

Counting in French

Learning objective
● To count to 10 in French.

Resources
'French' Notebook file; photocopiable page 169 'Counting in French', one for each child.

Links to other subjects
Mathematics
PNS: Counting and understanding number
● Counting in French can be linked to general work on counting.

Starter
Go to page 7 of the Notebook file. Practise counting to 20 in English. Read the numbers in order. Then use the Spotlight tool to move the spotlight over random numbers, out of sequence, getting the children to say the number as it appears. Roll the dice, and ask the children to say the number of spots they see.

Whole-class shared work
● Go to page 8. Count from 1 to 10 in French. Ask the children to listen carefully to what you say.
● Next, ask them to count in French with you. Focus on each number as you say it.
● Practise many times, allowing the children to recite the numbers without your guidance.
● Go to page 9 and ask the children *Combien?* (How many?) Invite a volunteer to say the number in French. If the rest of the class agree, they say *Vrai* (true); if they disagree, they say *Faux* (false).
● Count the number of dogs on the page in French. Use the Eraser from the Pen tray on the blue box to reveal the answer, and read it aloud. (The children do not need to read the words in French, but it is useful for them to hear the whole sentence in French.)
● Repeat this for pages 10, 11 and 12.

Independent work
● Organise the children into groups of three or four. Give a copy of photocopiable page 169 to each child.
● With adult support, encourage each group to count from 1 to 10 in French.
● Ask the children to play the game in pairs; the rest of the group are the judges.
● Each player picks a colour and takes it in turn to say a number in French. They should start on the bottom row of the photocopiable sheet and work their way up. If they say the number correctly, and the rest of the group agrees, they can colour in the circle. It is then the next player's turn. The first player to reach the top wins.
● If there is time, more than one game can be played.
● Monitor the groups closely to ensure that the less confident learners have the chance to say the numbers. Also ensure that all the children contribute in being judges for the two players.

Plenary
● Go to page 13. Play a class version of the game the children played in the independent activity. Split the class into two teams. Allow one member from each team to say one number at a time. Show them how to use the Fill Colour tool to colour in each hexagon as they progress up the page. The first team to reach the top is the winner.
● Praise the children in French – for example, *C'est bon! Magnifique! Très bien!*
● Go to page 14. Finish the lesson by asking each child to say their name and their age in French.

Whiteboard tools
Use the Spotlight tool to focus on one number at a time in the Starter.

 Pen tray

Fill Colour tool

Spotlight tool

Select tool

Name _____

Inside a Victorian home

■ Draw a picture of three different Victorian objects and write a sentence about them.

	This is a _____ It was used for
	This is a _____ It was used for
	This is a _____ It was used for

Toy detectives

- Sort your pictures of toys into 'old' and 'new'. Stick the pictures under the correct heading.

- Write a word to describe each toy. Use the word bank to help you.

Old toys	New toys

Word bank

modern	new	old	dirty
clean	broken	wood	plastic
rusty	metal	shiny	fabric

Getting from home to school

◼ Cut out these pictures and add them to your map.

◼ Use this word bank to help you label your map.

shop	park	flats	houses
church	mosque	synagogue	bridge
bus stop	footpath	road	river
trees	canal	railway	underpass
lollipop lady	zebra crossing	traffic light	

Illustrations © 2006, Jenny Tulip

◀◼ **SCHOLASTIC**

www.scholastic.co.uk

Our traffic survey

◼ The largest number of vehicles we spotted was:

◼ The smallest number of vehicles we spotted was:

◼ The noisiest vehicle was:

◼ The quietest vehicle was:

Fruit and vegetables

Name of fruit or vegetable	What does it feel like?	What does it smell like?	What does it taste like?	Did you like it?

Sliding picture

Rotating picture

The Nativity

My gift for Jesus is _____

I chose it because _____

Draw a picture of your gift for Jesus here:

▪SCHOLASTIC
www.scholastic.co.uk

Greeting someone in French

Illustrations © 2006, Jenny Tulip

Counting in French

■ Play the number game with a partner. Pick a colour each.

☐ Take turns to say a number in French. Start with the numbers in the bottom row.

☐ If you are right, colour the circle in your colour.

☐ You have to colour a path of hexagons from the bottom to the top. The first person to do this is the winner.

1	un	2	deux	3	trois	4	quatre	5	cinq
6	six	7	sept	8	huit	9	neuf	10	dix

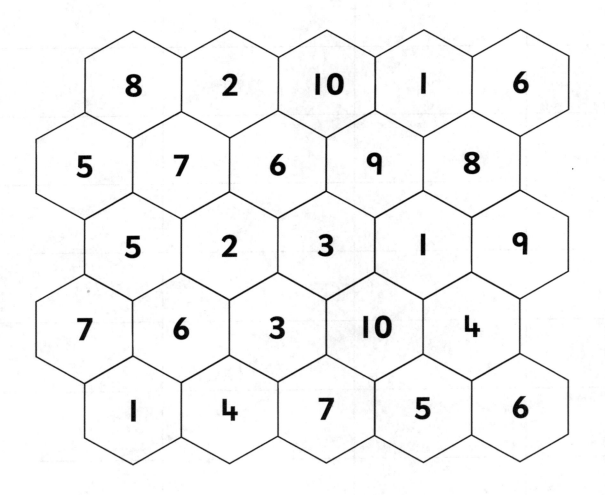

Whiteboard diary

Teacher's name: _____

Date	Subject/ Objective	How was the whiteboard used?	Evaluation

Whiteboard resources library

Teacher's name: _____

Name of resource and file location	Description of resource	How resource was used	Date resource was used

Using your SMART Board™ interactive whiteboard

This brief guide to using your SMART Board interactive whiteboard and Notebook software is based on the training manual *SMART Board Interactive Whiteboard Masters Learner Workbook* © SMART Technologies Inc.

Your finger is your mouse

You can control applications on your computer from the interactive whiteboard. A press with your finger on a SMART Board interactive whiteboard is the same as a click with your mouse. To open an application on your computer through the interactive whiteboard, double-press the icon with your finger in the same way that you would use a mouse to double-click on your desktop computer.

The SMART Pen tray

The SMART Pen tray consists of four colour-coded slots for Pens (black, red, green and blue) and one slot for the Eraser. Each slot has a sensor to identify when the Pens or the Eraser have been picked up. You can write with the Pens, or with your finger, as long as the pen slot is empty. Likewise, if you remove the Eraser from the slot you can use either it or your hand to erase your digital ink.

The Pen tray has at least two buttons. One button is used to launch the On-screen Keyboard and the second button is used to make your next touch on the interactive whiteboard a right-click. Some interactive whiteboards have a third button, which is used to access the Help Centre quickly.

The On-screen Keyboard

The On-screen Keyboard allows you to type or edit text in any application without leaving the interactive whiteboard. It can be accessed either by pressing the appropriate button in the Pen tray, or through the SMART Board tools menu (see page 173).

A dropdown menu allows you to select which keyboard you would like to use. The default Classic setting is a standard 'qwerty' keyboard. Select the Simple setting to arrange the keyboard in alphabetical order, as a useful facility for supporting younger or less confident learners. A Number pad is also available through the On-screen Keyboard.

The Fonts toolbar appears while you are typing or after you double-press a text object. Use it to format properties such as font size and colour.

On-screen Keyboard

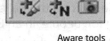

Floating tools toolbar

The Transparency layer

When you remove a Pen from the Pen tray, a border appears around your desktop and the Floating tools toolbar launches. The border indicates that the 'transparency layer' is in place and you can write on the desktop just as you would write on a transparent sheet, annotating websites, or any images you display. The transparency layer remains in place until all the Pens and the Eraser have been returned to the Pen tray. Your first touch of the board thereafter will remove the border and any notes or drawings you have made.

Ink Aware applications

When software is Ink Aware, you can write and draw directly into the active file. For example, if you write or draw something while using Microsoft Word, you can save your Word file and your notes will be visible the next time you open it. Ink Aware software includes the Microsoft applications Word, Excel, PowerPoint; graphic applications such as Microsoft Paint and Imaging; and other applications such as Adobe Acrobat. Ensure that the SMART Aware toolbar is activated by selecting View, then toolbars, and checking that the SMART Aware toolbar option is ticked.

Aware tools

When you are using Microsoft Word or Excel, you will now notice three new buttons that will be either integrated into your current toolbar (as shown on the left), or separated as a floating toolbar. Press the first button to insert your drawing or writing as an image directly into your document or spreadsheet. The second button converts writing to typed text and insert it directly into your document or spreadsheet. Press the third button to save a screen capture in Notebook software.

When you are using Microsoft PowerPoint on an interactive whiteboard, the SlideShow toolbar appears automatically. Use the left- and right-hand buttons on the SlideShow toolbar to navigate your presentation. Press the centre button to launch the Command menu for additional options, including access to the SMART Floating tools (see page 175), and the facility to save notes directly into your presentation.

SlideShow toolbar

SMART Board tools

The SMART Board tools include functions that help you to operate the interactive whiteboard more effectively. Press the SMART Board icon at the bottom right of your screen to access the menu.

- SMART Recorder: Use this facility to make a video file of anything you do on the interactive whiteboard. You can then play the recording on any computer with SMART Video player or Windows® Media Player.
- Floating tools: The features you use most are included in the Floating toolbar. It can also be customised to incorporate any tools. Press the More button at the bottom-right of the toolbar and select Customise Floating Tools from the menu. Select a tool from the Available Tools menu and press Add to include it.
- Start Centre: This convenient toolbar gives you access to the most commonly used SMART Board interactive whiteboard tools.
- Control Panel: Use the Control Panel to configure a variety of software and hardware options for your SMART Board and software.

See page 175 for a visual guide to the SMART Board tools.

Using SMART Notebook™ software

Notebook software is SMART's whiteboard software. It can be used as a paper notebook to capture notes and drawings, and also enables you to insert multimedia elements like images and interactive resources.

Side tabs
There are three tabs on the right-hand side of the Notebook interface:

Page Sorter: The Page Sorter tab allows you to see a thumbnail image of each page in your Notebook file. The active page is indicated by a dropdown menu and a blue border around the thumbnail image. Select the dropdown menu for options including Delete page, Insert blank page, Clone page and Rename page. To change the page order, select a thumbnail and drag it to a new location within the order.

Gallery: The Gallery contains thousands of resources to help you quickly develop and deliver lessons in rich detail. Objects from the Gallery can be useful visual prompts; for example, searching for 'people' in an English lesson will bring up images that could help build pupils' ideas for verbs and so on. Objects you have created yourself can also be saved into the Gallery for future use, by dragging them into the My Content folder.

The Search facility in the Gallery usually recognises words in their singular, rather than plural, form. Type 'interactive' or 'flash' into the Gallery to bring up a bank of interactive resources for use across a variety of subjects including mathematics, science, music and design and technology.

Attachments: The Attachments tab allows you to link to supporting documents and webpages directly from your Notebook file. To insert a file, press the Insert button at the bottom of the tab and browse to the file location, or enter the internet address.

Objects in Notebook software
Anything you select inside the work area of a Notebook page is an object. This includes text, drawing or writing, shapes created with the drawing tools, or content from the Gallery, your computer, or the internet.

(ii)

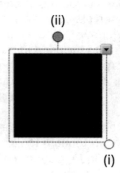

(i)

Manipulating objects: To resize an object, select it and drag the white handle (i). Use the green handle (ii) to rotate an object. To adjust the properties of a selected object, use the dropdown menu.

- Locking: This sub-menu includes options to 'Lock in place', which means that the object cannot be moved or altered in any way. Alternatively you can choose to 'Allow Move' or 'Allow Move and Rotate', which mean that your object cannot be resized.
- Grouping: Select two or more objects by pressing and dragging your finger diagonally so that the objects are surrounded by a selection box. Press the dropdown menu and choose Grouping > Group. If you want to separate the objects, choose Grouping > Ungroup.
- Order: Change the order in which objects are layered by selecting 'Bring forward' or 'Send backward' using this option.
- Infinite Cloner: Select 'Infinite Cloner' to reproduce an object an unlimited number of times.
- Properties: Use this option to change the colour, line properties and transparency of an object.
- Handwriting recognition: If you have written something with a Pen tool, you can convert it to text by selecting it and choosing the Recognise option from the dropdown menu.

Tools glossary

Notebook tools
Hints and tips
● Move the toolbar to the bottom of the screen to make it more accessible for children.

● Gradually reveal information to your class with the Screen Shade.

● Press the Full screen button to view everything on an extended Notebook page.

● Use the Capture tool to take a screenshot of work in progress, or completed work, to another page and print this out.

● Type directly into a shape created with the Shapes tool by double-pressing it and using the On-screen Keyboard.

	Pen tray		Lines tool
	Next page		Shapes tool
	Previous page		Text tool
	Blank Page button		Fill Colour tool
	Open		Transparency tool
	Save		Line properties
	Paste		Move toolbar to the top
	Undo button		
	Redo button		Capture tool
	Delete button		Area Capture tool
	Screen Shade		Area Capture 2
	Full screen		Area Capture 3
	Select tool		Area Capture (freehand) tool
	Pen tool		
	Highlighter pen		Page Sorter
	Creative pen		Gallery
	Eraser tool		Attachments

SMART Board tools
Hints and tips
● Use the SMART recorder to capture workings and methods, and play them back to the class for discussion in the Plenary.

● Adjust the shape and transparency of the Spotlight tool when focusing on elements of an image.

● Customise the Floating tools to incorporate any tools that you regularly use. Press the More button at the bottom right of the toolbar and select Customise Floating Tools from the menu.

Press the SMART Board icon at the bottom right of your screen to access the **SMART Board tools** menu (shown right).

The **Start Centre** (shown below), is reached through the SMART Board tools menu.

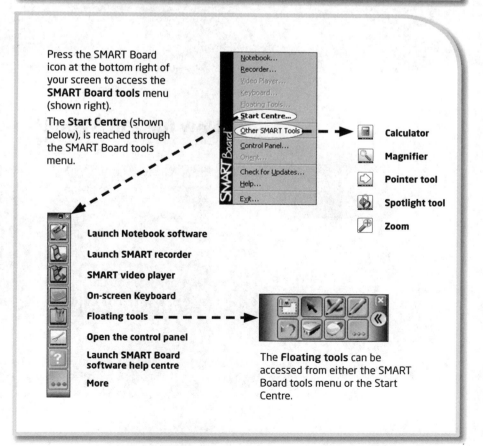

Launch Notebook software

Launch SMART recorder

SMART video player

On-screen Keyboard

Floating tools

Open the control panel

Launch SMART Board software help centre

More

The **Floating tools** can be accessed from either the SMART Board tools menu or the Start Centre.

Calculator

Magnifier

Pointer tool

Spotlight tool

Zoom